# IS
# GUINNESS
# GOOD
# FOR YOU?

The Bid for Distillers — The Inside Story

# PETER PUGH

First published in Great Britain 1987 by Financial Training Publications Limited, Holland House, 140–144 Freston Road, London W10 6TR

ISBN: 1 85185 074 0

Typeset by Kerrypress Ltd, Luton
Printed by Redwood Burn Ltd, Trowbridge

# CONTENTS

# ACKNOWLEDGEMENTS

In writing a contentious book I have spoken to many people who would not thank me for thanking them publicly. The people who have helped me know that I am very grateful.

I would like to thank publicly, Peter Simcock who helped with the drafts; The Grand Hotel, Eastbourne, where much of the book was written; Financial Training Publications who gave much help and encouragement and who moved with remarkable speed to produce the book quickly; William Shakespeare who showed that ambition and the blind lust for power were not twentieth century phenomena; and Magnus Spence who drew the cartoons.

# PICTURE CREDITS

1, 4, 9, 11, 12, 13, 14, 15, 21, 22, 23, 24, 27, 31, 32, 34, 35, 37, 40
*Universal Pictorial Press and Agency Ltd*

2, 16, 26
*Syndication International (1986) Ltd*

18, 19, 20, 30, 36, 38, 39, 41, 42, 43
*The Press Association Ltd*

29
*Associated Newspapers Group*

5, 44
*Desmond O'Neill Features*

45
*Financial Times*

*Others came from various sources including Scottish Business Insider.*

# DRAMATIS PERSONAE

## The Family in the Company

| | |
|---|---|
| Benjamin Guinness, Lord Iveagh | chairman of Guinness from 1962 to 1986, now president |
| Viscount Boyd of Merton | resigned as director early 1986 |
| Jonathan Guinness | director |
| Edward Guinness | director |

## The Saunders

| | |
|---|---|
| Ernest Saunders *† | chief executive and from July 1986 chairman of Guiness |
| Carole Saunders | wife of Ernest Saunders |
| Emanuel Schleyer | father of Ernest Saunders |
| Johanna Schleyer | mother of Ernest Saunders |

## The Executive Guinness Board in 1986

Lord Iveagh
Jonathan Guinness
Edward Guinness
Ernest Saunders
Victor Steel
Shaun Dowling
Brian Baldock

## The First Non-Executive Board

| | |
|---|---|
| Thomas Ward*† | American lawyer |
| Olivier Roux*† | consultant from Bain and Co. |
| Artur Furer† | Swiss banker |

ix

Dramatis Personae

## The Second Non-Executive Board
### (appointed Summer and Autumn 1986)

| | |
|---|---|
| Sir Norman Macfarlane | chairman of Macfarlane Group (clansman) |
| Sir David Plaistow | chairman of Vickers |
| Ian Maclaurin | · chairman of Tesco |
| Anthony Greener | managing director of Dunhill |
| Ian Chapman | chairman, William Collins |

## The Bankers

| | |
|---|---|
| Sir Peter Carey | chairman, Morgan Grenfell |
| Christopher Reeves† | chief executive, Morgan Grenfell |
| Graham Walsh† | head of corporate finance, Morgan Grenfell |
| Roger Seelig*† | corporate finance director, Morgan Grenfell |
| Tony Richmond-Watson | director, Morgan Grenfell |
| Sir John Nott | chairman, Lazards |
| Marcus Agius | director, Lazards |
| Lord Rockley | director, Kleinwort Benson |
| Ian Macintosh | chief executive, Samuel Montagu |
| Rupert Faure-Walker | director, Samuel Montagu |
| Lord Spens† | head of corporate finance, Henry Ansbacher |
| Richard Fenhalls | managing director, Henry Ansbacher |
| John Chiene | joint chief executive, Hill Samuel and Co. |

## Other Guinness Advisers

| | |
|---|---|
| David Mayhew* | partner, Cazenove (stockbrokers) |
| Anthony Salz* | partner, Freshfields (lawyers) |

x

Dramatis Personae

## Distillers Board

| | |
|---|---|
| John Connell | chairman |
| David Connell | director |
| Bill Spengler | deputy chairman |
| Sir Nigel Broackes | non-executive director |

## Argyll Board

| | |
|---|---|
| James Gulliver | chairman |
| Alistair Grant | chief executive |
| David Webster | finance director |

## The Scots

| | |
|---|---|
| Sir Thomas Risk | Governor of Bank of Scotland (proposed chairman of Guinness) |
| Charles Fraser | partner W. & J. Burness (WS) chairman of Morgan Grenfell (Scotland), director of Bell's (post Guinness takeover) (proposed director of Guinness) |
| Raymond Miquel | chairman of Bell's |
| Peter Tyrie | director of Bell's |
| Angus Grossart | chairman of Noble Grossart (merchant bank) |
| Peter Stevenson | ex-director, Noble Grossart |
| Alick Rankin | chief executive, Scottish and Newcastle Breweries |
| Malcolm Rifkind | Minister of State, Scotland |
| Raymond Johnstone | chairman, Murray Johnstone (fund managers in Glasgow) |
| Graeme Knox | general manager, Investments, Scottish Amicable |
| Bill Walker | MP for North Tayside |
| Sir Alex Fletcher | MP and adviser to James Gulliver |

Dramatis Personae

## The Public Relations Teams

Peter Gummer — chairman, Shandwick
Brian Basham — chairman, Broad Street Group
Roddy Dewe — chairman, Dewe Rogerson
Sir Gordon Reece — former public relations adviser to Mrs Thatcher, adviser to Saunders
Tony Good — chairman, Good Relations
Peter Binns — chairman, Binns Cornwall
David Wynne Morgan — managing director, Hill and Knowlton

## Journalists

Kenneth Fleet — *The Times*
Ivan Fallon — *Sunday Times*
Alf Young — *Glasgow Herald* (formerly of *The Scotsman*)
Alex Murray — *Sunday Telegraph*
Melvyn Marckus — *The Observer*
Andrew Alexander — *Daily Mail*
Peter Koenig — *Euromoney* (formerly of *Institutional Investor*)

## Lawyers

Jeremy Lever, QC — specialist in mergers and acquisitions
John Swift, QC — specialist in mergers and acquisitions
Sir David Napley — specialist in criminal law

## Others

Lord Weinstock — managing director, GEC
Sir Robin Leigh Pemberton — Governor of the Bank of England
Sir Nicholas Goodison — chairman, Stock Exchange
Michael Dee — director of Mergers and Acquisitions Consultants, Jersey

xii

Dramatis Personae

| Paul Channon | Secretary of State, Trade and Industry |
| Michael Howard | Minister, Consumer Affairs |
| David Barker | investment manager, Norwich Union (now with Hill Samuel) |

## The Recipients of Fees

| Gerald Ronson | chairman, Heron International |
| Sir Jack Lyons† | UK representative, Bain and Co. |
| Tony Parnes† | 'half-commission' man with Alexanders, Laing and Cruickshank |
| Ephraim Margulies | chairman, S. & W. Berisford |

## The Americans

| Ivan Boesky | the disgraced arbitrageur |
| Meshulam Riklis | chief executive, Schenley and Co. |
| Pia Zadora | wife of Riklis |

## The DTI Inspectors

| David Donaldson, QC | lawyer |
| Ian Watt | partner in Thomson, McLintock |

* *Members of Guinness 'War Cabinet' during Distillers bid*
† *Those who have resigned, or have been asked to resign since 1 December 1986*

*Dedication*

*To Felicity*

# PREFACE

**'If it were done when 'tis done, then 'twere well it were done quickly'**

The interest in the Guinness 'scandal' has been intense, not only in financial and business circles, but throughout the whole population. That is not surprising — it is a story of naked greed, lust for power, vaulting ambition, discovery and skulduggery on an international scale.

It is not often that we are 'in the right place at the right time', but in this case I happened to be. I knew some of the leaders of the financial community in Edinburgh and they were intimately involved in both the takeover of Bell's and of Distillers and, of course, in the Thomas Risk affair.

It was important to try and produce as balanced a book as possible, and though I have not been able to talk to everyone involved, I have certainly spoken to participants on all sides of the seemingly unending controversies.

I have found the research and writing quite fascinating. I hope you will find the result interesting and perhaps stimulating.

Peter Pugh
March 1987

# ONE

## The Dynasts

In 1756 Dr Arthur Price, Archbishop of Cashel, left this world to take up his rightful—and eternal—place in a better one. The grief to his household caused by his passing away was ameliorated slightly by the munificence of his will: if the good Doctor had gone to receive his just reward in heaven, then his servants and retainers were to receive a foretaste of Christian bounty whilst still on this earth. What became of the bulk of the Archbishop's estate can doubtless be traced by those of an inquisitive mind, but the fate of the £100 he left to his brewer, Arthur Guinness, provided the basis for an economic enterprise which has probably given the world more pleasure and practical interest than the remainder of the Archbishop's bequests combined. For with that £100 Arthur was able to buy his first modest brewery, at Leixlip in County Kildare.

The first Guinness brewery prospered modestly, if not

1

spectacularly, and provided sufficient profit for Arthur to acquire a somewhat run-down second brewery at James's Gate in Dublin. The capital that Arthur took over was less than inspiring—a dwelling house, two malt houses and a venerable copper brewing vessel—but it had two major attractions; the first was its annual rent of £45 on a 9,000 year lease, and the second was its access to the waters of the River Liffey, reckoned then to be a superior ingredient for ales and table beer (the world famous Guinness porter—or stout, as it is more commonly known—was not produced until 1796).

Two small breweries in the Dublin area hardly made Arthur Guinness a gentleman of note in late eighteenth century Ireland, even amongst his fellow brewers. However, he had energy and ambition enough to become warden of the Dublin Corporation of Brewers in 1760, and sufficient personal attraction to take the hand of Olivia Whitmore, a Dublin heiress, in 1761. The Whitmore fortune allied to the Guinness enterprise made for a solid foundation upon which a thriving business could be built. In 1770, Arthur Guinness was elected Master of the Brewer's Corporation, and official brewer to Dublin Castle, the Irish seat of government. Both of these positions carried power and influence, which Arthur used unashamedly in 1773 when the Corporation of the City of Dublin accused him—justifiably—of damaging City property in order to obtain water from the River Liffey above and beyond the amount stipulated in his lease. A compromise was soon reached, whereby Arthur became a tenant of the Corporation for a rent of £10 a year, and was allowed to draw as much water as he pleased.

By 1789, when Arthur was 64, his James's Gate brewery had expanded beyond all recognition, he had diversified to the tune of £8,000 into the flour milling business, and was coming to be a force to be recognised in Dublin's commercial society. He was also known for his good health, enormous energy, and equally prodigious virility. He fathered 21 children by Olivia (the first when she was only 19) of whom only 10 survived. Upon his death in 1803, aged 78, he left a personal estate valued at around £23,000, a thriving brewery and a product that was to become internationally famous—Guinness Stout.

## The Origin of Guinness

The exact origins of Guinness's famous porter are as obscured by legend as the originals of any popular beverage, be it tea or champagne.

In fact porter, made by adding hops to malted barley and then fermenting the boiled mixture with yeast, had been drunk in London since at least the 1650s. What differentiated Guinness stout from any of its many rivals remains a matter of conjecture. Some purists consider that the key lies in the use of water from the Liffey. Connoisseurs in Ireland's twin capitals, Dublin and Liverpool (as everyone knows, a pipeline runs directly from the James's Gate brewery to a secret terminal at Seaforth docks!) would drink bottled Guinness before they would touch the stuff available on draught from Malaysia, Canada, Trinidad or any of the several other nations which now brew Guinness. West Africans, on the other hand, gingerly sipping the stout within a stone's throw of London's Park Royal brewery, do so only in homage to the brew's true spiritual homeland— the great Guinness brewery in Nigeria.

Whatever may be the appeal of Guinness stout, the drink is perhaps something more than a mere alcoholic beverage. It is an institution, a piece of folklore, and a drink which inspires fierce loyalties, strong antipathies, and the type of snobbery usually only associated with wine. Indeed, its enigmatic qualities have ensured that it was ever thus. Its powers as a restorative were remarked upon by officers in the Napoleonic wars; in 1837 the young Disraeli wrote to his sister of dining at the Carlton 'of oysters, broiled bones and Guinness'; and— perhaps the supreme accolade—the brief produced by the advertising agency that came up with the 'pure genius' campaign was such a masterpiece of pretentiousness that it appeared in *Private Eye's* Pseud's Corner.

However, discovering why people should have developed a taste for what was rapidly becoming Ireland's foremost stout was of little concern to the first Arthur Guinness or his chosen successor in the brewery business, his second son, born in 1768 and also called Arthur*. Their only concern was how to take advantage of this phenomenon, and with their characteristic energy, commercial shrewdness and political discretion—always a necessary virtue in Ireland—take advantage they did. The James's Gate brewery had an annual output of just over 10,000 gallons in its first few years: by 1805,

---

*The first Arthur Guinness's eldest son, Hosea, did not take up a place in the family business; instead, he chose to enter the Church, which carried a good deal more social respectability than 'mere commerce' in the eighteenth century.

two years after the first Arthur's death, this had grown to 350,000 gallons, a 350 per cent increase in less than 50 years.

## The Growth of the Empire

One of the major factors behind this phenomenal growth was, strangely enough, the French Revolutionary and Napoleonic Wars (1793 to 1815). Guinness porter found a new market in the increasing numbers of soldiery stationed in Ireland, and war brought with it a degree of prosperity to all classes in Ireland. It also brought with it a surge of patriotism, and porter became a replacement, although never a substitute, for imported French wines and brandies. This otherwise turbulent period saw a sixfold increase in the sales of Guinness porter.

Indeed, to adopt a phrase, what was bad for Ireland was not necessarily bad for Guinness: the brewery seemed to thrive on the adversity of the nation. One of the most sustained periods of growth in the company's history occurred during the horrors of the 'Potato Famine', when the failure of the 1845 to 1850 potato crops led to the degeneration of Ireland into the most miserable country in Europe, reducing its population from eight to six million—either by death or emigration. This agrarian disaster had little effect on the mercantile economy of Dublin: paradoxically, the City enjoyed a certain prosperity, and fortunes were made either from the import of grain or the export of the wretched Irish peasantry. Equally, grain had become too valuable a commodity to be used in the distilling of whiskey, and the resulting shortage of that spirit led to the increased consumption of porter. This was now the major product of the Guinness brewery and it began to achieve an all-Irish market, whereas hitherto it had been limited largely to the Dublin area.

In fact, prior to the 1850s, Guinness stout enjoyed a higher regard—and from 1840 onwards higher sales—in England than it did in Ireland. Arthur and his younger brother Benjamin had introduced the product into England in the early part of the nineteenth century via Bristol and Liverpool. This penetration of the English market was facilitated by three factors. One was the undeniable superiority of Irish porter over its English counterpart: this was due to the widespread use of Patent Brown Malt in Ireland, which produced a consistently high quality beverage. Secondly, from 1824 onwards Irish brewers were able to ship their products to England via steam vessels, which reduced the transport time from two weeks to two days. However, superior brewing techniques and higher shipping costs should logically lead to higher prices in what was, effectively, an overseas market. This is where the third factor in Guinness's favour came into play: Irish brewers were past masters at evading the excise duty on malt purchases and as such they were able to undersell English brewers in their domestic market.

The second Arthur Guinness, who had worked so hard to build on his father's success, died in 1855 aged 87. He left behind him a record of solid achievement and an impeccable reputation as the archetypal businessman of the Industrial Revolution—one eye to God, and the other to the main chance. He was succeeded by his youngest son Benjamin, already 57 by the time of Arthur's death, who had been working in the brewery since he was 15. Although Benjamin's time as head of the business was short in contrast to that of his father and grandfather, a mere 13 years from 1855 to 1868, it was a highly significant one in terms of the assimilation of the family into the realms of social honour and national politics.

## Into the Aristocracy

Benjamin's path to the elevation of the Guinness family from prosperous, successful but socially insignificant 'tradesmen' to an aristocratic dynasty was fourfold: the support of the Established Church in Ireland, the purchase of some of the most prestigious Irish houses and estates, an entry into politics, and marriage into an aristocracy that eyed the Guinness fortune with interest. All of this was, of course, underpinned by the continuing success of the family's breweries and the pints of porter they produced.

In 1851, Benjamin was elected Lord Mayor of Dublin and inaugurated amidst much ceremony. 'From this position of mercantile power and affluence he set out to broaden and elevate the base of what could by now truly be conceived as a dynasty invested with the promise of a brilliant succession.* He considered his present estates insufficient reflection of the importance of the man who would head Ireland's single largest business: his solution to this was to purchase the town mansion built in 1746 by the rich and worldly Bishop of

*The Silver Salver, Frederic Mullally (Granda Publishing Ltd, 1981)

Clogher, on St Stephen's Green, one of the largest city squares in Europe. In 1856 he spent £150,000 of his own fortune to restore Dublin's Anglican Cathedral, St Patrick's. This was to be the scene of the wedding of his daughter Anne to the Honourable William Coyningham, later to become the fourth Baron Plunket, thus bringing the first title into the family.

The act of public and pious generosity of the restoration of St Patrick's was counterbalanced by the acquisition of the stunningly beautiful Ashford Estate in County Galway which, combined with the St Anne's estate close to Dublin, made Benjamin a landowner of some substance in an age when land was still the true mark of a gentleman. And as if to stress his roots—real or imagined—in Ireland's heroic past, he adopted as the Guinness emblem the harp of Bryan Boru, one of that nation's legendary warrior-kings.

Benjamin's political leanings were the usual mixture of honest principle and understandable self-interest that characterised a pre-ideological age when political service was seen as a duty rather than an end in itself. The sheer economic strength the Guinness breweries provided allowed him to pin the family's political colours to the mast, something his discreet forebearers had been reluctant to do in an often viciously sectarian Ireland. Those colours were the orange and blue of Toryism, Union, and the religious Establishment in Ireland, which faced the twin threats of the fiery and devout William Gladstone and the nascent Sinn Fein. In 1865 Benjamin was elected as the Conservative MP for Dublin, and he took his fight against Gladstone's Liberalism to the House of Commons.

In fact, Benjamin was the first head of the great brewing families in Great Britain and Ireland to attack the Liberals. Prior to him, the support of the brewers, and their funds, had gone to the Liberals, who were considered to be the party of free trade and industry. Benjamin had detected a worrying element in Gladstone's politics—temperance. Given the basis of the family fortune, which no amount of rural acreage could ever replace, Benjamin's antipathy to Gladstone was only natural, even if the latter had not been in favour of the disestablishment of the Church of Ireland. In any event, Gladstone's government fell in 1867, and Benjamin was ennobled with a baronetcy by way of reward.

In the tradition of the first two Arthurs, Benjamin had directed the affairs of the brewery almost entirely from Dublin. Under his direction the family business had grown to such an extent that its output of porter equalled the combined production of its 10 major competitors in Dublin: indeed, its annual output of 11,250,000 gallons was only exceeded by four breweries operating in the much bigger market of the British mainland.

Upon the death of Benjamin in 1868, control of the family business devolved upon his youngest son, Edward, who like Benjamin had begun work in the brewery at the age of 15. Edward had in fact been named as a partner in the business with his eldest brother, Arthur. However, Arthur's twin passions for politics and social advancement, coupled with no great managerial talent, led to Edward buying him out for £686,000 in 1876 (about the equivalent of £20 million today). This amicable arrangement left both men with ample time to pursue their interest; Arthur went in search of a peerage (which he eventually acquired) and Edward carried on running a highly successful brewing empire.

This Edward did with conspicuous success, possessing a shrewd, practical intelligence that made him a master of detail and a formidable businessman. Nor was he without social aspirations—in 1875, he purchased and restored the mansion of Farmleigh which he considered to be a suitable seat for the Earldom which he felt certain would one day be his. Until that day came, however, Edward would not neglect the management of the brewery which would make it all possible.

## Guinness goes Public

In 1885, Edward received his baronetcy, which came as no great surprise to anybody. In October of the next year, he did something that was—he announced that Arthur Guinness Son and Co. was going public. There was uproar on the floors of the London and Dublin Stock Exchanges, but whilst the uproar in London settled down into a more decorous joy, in Dublin it took on a bitter note: no prospectuses were sent to Dublin stockbrokers inviting them to participate in the new £6 million company. The blame for this was firmly attached to Baring and Co., the brokers handling the operation, and they were guilty of a cavalierness that bordered on the illegal.

Not surprisingly, the £4 million worth of shares on offer (Sir Edward had stated that he would keep a third of the share capital for himself and his family) was hugely oversubscribed. Matters were not helped by the allocation of shares decided upon by Baring and Co.;

they retained £850,000 worth for themselves, allocated another £850,000 worth to 20 of their favoured subscribers, and a further £1.5 million went to 50 London stockbroking firms. The majority of ordinary investors went away empty-handed from what should have been the share launch of the decade, and Barings were severely admonished by the Committee of the Stock Exchange. Guinness's first foray onto the floor of the Stock Exchange was coloured, ominously enough, by scandal.

The most disappointed and badly treated would-be investors were, of course, those members of the Irish public who had not even been invited to apply. On a brighter note, however, the Guinness workforce did very well out of the launch. To celebrate the company going public Sir Edward gave each worker in the brewery's commercial department a bonus worth three months' salary, whilst draymen and other manual workers received the equivalent of a month's wages. This gesture cost Sir Edward £60,000, and reinforced the Guinness reputation of benevolence to its workforce.

In fact, such benevolence was not confined to those few who were fortunate to work for Guinness. Even in an age where the wealthy capitalist was expected as part of his Christian duty to donate to worthy causes and the deserving poor, Sir Edward set some remarkably open-handed standards. His most supreme act of generosity, the benefits of which are still being felt today all over Great Britain and Ireland, was the establishment in 1886 of the Guinness Trust for the Housing of the Poor (which continues today as the Guinness Housing Association). Sir Edward had placed the then phenomenal sum of £250,000 with three trustees, who were instructed to provide superior housing at moderate cost for 'the labouring poor' in London and Dublin. Two years later, Sir Edward was elevated to the peerage of Baron Iveagh of County Down; the title was in recognition of his generosity, but it would be overly cynical to suggest that it was, in effect, a direct purchase—indeed, such a transaction would probably have come a great deal cheaper.

## The First Absentee Landlord

Edward was the first head of the company to spend more of his time in England than in Ireland: indeed, after 1890, he was to all intents and purposes a resident of England. This was for any number of reasons: doubtless the growing pressure for home rule in Ireland was not to his

8

political taste; equally, the social advancement he craved as his rightful reward could more easily be obtained entertaining the very best of society—including King George V—on his extensive Elveden estate in East Anglia. Probably most important, however, was that England, or more properly London, was the heart of the company's commercial empire. Edward may have been a generous benefactor and as eager to court social advancement as any man to whom mere monetary rewards have lost some of their significance, but he was also a first rate businessman. Under his stewardship, the Dublin brewery, covering some 500 acres, became the largest in the world, and between 1906 and 1919 company profits more than doubled from £1,036,305 to £2,175,816. This astonishing achievement was made all the more remarkable when one considers the compulsory reduction in the brewery's output during the 1914–18 war, and the introduction for the first time (as a 'temporary war-time measure') of licensing hours.

In 1919, when the endless stream of dark, bitter beer had made him one of the richest men in England, Edward received his reward for services to industry, the public, and the amusement of the cream of English society. He was ennobled as the Earl of Iveagh and Viscount Elveden, an honour which, by the canons of his day, he richly deserved. His latter years until his death in 1927 were spent in extending and developing the labyrinthine network of family trusts, as much a Guinness tradition as brewing fine stout, which supported the family in the fabulous manner which they now considered to be their birthright. Upon his death, a few weeks before his 80th birthday, flags flew at half-mast in Dublin, and the Tory party, at its annual conference in Cardiff, observed a minute's silence for their generous patron. Many felt that the passing away of this great Victorian businessman left a special gap in their lives—his employees had lost a benevolent master, the English social scene a charming and generous host. Arguably, however, the greatest loss would be felt by the brewing empire which three generations had created; Edward and his forebears had had a touch of greatness about them—the next two generations were merely competent. That was sufficient when all was going well; when it was not, when circumstances changed, they lacked the native ability to work their own way out of the situation.

The career of Rupert Edward, 2nd Earl of Iveagh as head of the family business marks something of a golden age in the company's history, a final flowering of its energies that established it as a truly international entity. It remains a moot point, however, whether this was because of, or in spite of, the man at its helm. Rupert was born in 1874, and was 53 when he succeeded to his father's title and the head of Arthur Guinness Sons & Co. Ltd. Prior to that he had enjoyed an undistinguished parliamentary career, first as MP for South East Essex from 1912 to 1918, and then for Southend on Sea, which was something of a Guinness family fief, until 1927.

The 2nd Earl would not have been afraid to admit that his talents as a politician were limited. He was to earn much greater fame as an experimental farmer of some note—he played a significant part in the development of land reclamation techniques—and as the man who gave the world the first Guinness advertisements. Prior to 1928 there had been little, if any, advertising by the company. Indeed, there had been no reason why they should: sales of Guinness stout seemed to multiply in an almost geometric progression, and the company's main problem was to satisfy, not stimulate, demand. Whilst this situation held, the socially sensitive Guinness family saw no reason to emphasise their commercial origins and continued dependence upon the thirst of the working classes of Great Britain, Ireland and the Empire.

**The First Real Advertising**

Rupert, a more pragmatic and innovative man who—to his credit—seemed largely unconcerned with such subtle social niceties, saw no reason why the company should not advertise the putative qualities of its stout. Concerned with falling sales caused by the onset of the 'great depression' he approved a limited experimental poster campaign in Scotland. This campaign had shown promise, and a year later, in 1929, it was extended to England. Rupert had insisted that the campaign copy should be 'clean and wholesome'—after all, if he had to publicise his commercial background then he might as well stress the beneficial nature of his product—and thus was born the immortal slogan 'Guinness is Good for You'. Sales figures rose in line with the campaign and the company became firm advocates of advertising, setting creative standards for the next 50 years to which most other companies—or rather their advertising agencies—could only aspire.

Undoubtedly, Guinness advertising played its part in cushioning the company from the worst blows of the great depression, and with the upturn in the economy from the mid 1930s onwards its huge resources and natural resilience once gain made it a 'blue chip' investment with its shareholders. It was the Second World War, however, and the changes it wrought in economic and social relationships that was to prove a watershed in the company's history.

Whatever may have been the fate of the company, the Guinness family can by no stretch of the imagination be said to have had a 'good' war. On the business side, prospects were excellent; demand from a thirsty labour force stretched the brewery's capacity to the utmost. Nevertheless, there was still sufficient for the company to indulge in one of those acts of generosity—half-magnanimity and half public relations coup—which had become its hallmark; at Christmas 1939, 159,000 bottles of Guinness were sent to the British expeditionary force in France.*

It was in personal terms that the family, and perhaps the business, suffered its greatest losses. The first was that of Rupert's youngest brother, Walter, a man who had served with gallantry and distinction in both the Boer War and World War I. In November 1944, at the age of 64 and ennobled as Lord Moyne, he was continuing his life of public service as Minister Resident in the Middle East, with responsibility for an area extending from Iran to Libya. He was retiring to his official residence one lunchtime when he was assassinated by gunmen from the Zionist Stern gang.

It was a cruel blow to the Guinness family, made all the more senseless by the fact that it did little to advance the Zionist cause even in Israel, where the murder was roundly condemned by all save the members of the Stern and Irgun gangs. But there was a greater tragedy still to come. The Guinness succession lay with Rupert's only surviving son, Arthur Onslow Edward, Viscount Elveden. Arthur had held a commission in the Territorial Army since the early 1930s, and had taken up a regular commission in an infantry regiment after the Munich crisis of 1938. A brave and conscientious soldier—he had gone on to serve in an anti-tank regiment—he was killed in action on 14th February 1945. It was just over three months since the murder of his uncle; it was just under three months to the end of the war.

Arthur's tragic death threatened the Guinness tradition of a direct male descendant being chairman of the company. The Earl of Iveagh

---

*It is interesting to note that this idea was picked up by Coca-Cola who, upon America's entry to the war in December 1941, decreed that no GI should be more than an hour away from a Coke, regardless of where in the world he happened to be. With the invasion of France in 1944, Coca-Cola bottling plants were actually set up within five miles of the front line.

was now 71 and, although enjoying good health, would not live forever. Arthur's son and heir, Arthur Benjamin, now also heir to the family title, was a boy of eight. However, the remarkable longevity of the old Earl, who died in 1967 at the age of 93, ensured that the tradition was carried on. The survival of the tradition was also due in no small part to the precocious maturity and sense of duty of the young Arthur Benjamin, known as Ben to his intimates, who felt himself capable of heading the company when his grandfather stepped down at the age of 88.

## Ben Becomes Chairman

A modest, self-effacing and thoughtful young man, Ben found himself at the age of 25 as chairman of one of Britain's greatest public companies, controlling a trading empire with a stock market valuation in 1961 of £87 million. In 1963 Ben married Miranda Smiley, who, after presenting him with two daughters, finally gave birth to a son in 1969. The dynasty, it seemed, had been secured.

Before we leave the Guinness family to concentrate on the Guinness company we should perhaps note the irony of the fact that one member of the dynasty, Bryan Walter, Lord Moyne made a strong stand against that most potent of the modern marketing man's weapons, commercial television. In November 1953 he told the *Sunday Graphic*: 'If we have commercial television and our competitors, or the soft drink concerns, started advertising, we'd have to consider doing the same. This might force us to raise our prices or reduce our profits . . ..' Not much chance of convincing the institutions that you are the ace marketing company with that approach!

# TWO

## The Gentlemen Make Way
## for the Players

In the 20 years since Arthur Benjamin, from 1967 and 3rd Lord Iveagh, became the chairman of Guinness, something had gone drastically wrong. In 1961, the company's stock market valuation had stood at £87 million: in 1981 it was a little over £90 million. Pre-tax profits were almost stagnant at £42 million and the share price had slumped to 49 pence. It was observed that Guinness had gone through the stage of being a sleeping giant and was well on the way to becoming a dying dwarf. What had happened?

The painful and inescapable conclusion must be that Guinness' decline over this period was the result of failure at the very top: we can only conclude that of all those members of the Guinness family who ran the company, none of them was actually very good at management. And it must be stressed that the whole business was still very much a family affair: in 1979, the Guinness family had 9 members out of 22 on the board—this compared with seven representatives of the Marks and Sieff family on the 26-man board of Marks and Spencer.

Frederic Mullally, the unofficial chronicler of the Guinness family, asserts that the 3rd Earl of Iveagh had been 'groomed . . . as fastidiously as the heir to any royal family' to occupy the Guinness throne.* Hindsight and the most superficial of examinations of the company's fortunes during this period would tend to disprove that assertion. That the young Arthur Benjamin had been groomed for his responsibilities, both social and commercial, one cannot doubt: Eton and Trinity, Cambridge on the one hand, and long hours in the James's Gate and Park Royal breweries on the other, gave him a solid enough background. It also inculcated within him the great Guinness tradition of being traditional. This was not a managerial philosophy with which to approach the latter part of the twentieth century.

Guinness' major problem lay in its overall strategic orientation. The company had always been very sensitive to the fact that its manufacturing bases were far too narrow, that its heavy reliance on brewing made it extremely vulnerable. Its response to this was a strategy of diversification, which had its origins under the 2nd Earl, Rupert Edward. Given the realities of the situation, there was nothing wrong, *per se*, with such a strategy: its failure lay in its execution rather than its conception. What the company should have done was initiate a thorough and comprehensive marketing audit to identify what strengths could be capitalised upon, and what opportunities existed to be exploited. Such an audit would have revealed two very significant facts, one patently obvious and one only slightly less so.

The first of these was that the company's experience and expertise lay almost entirely in its brewing activities; through Guinness stout it had achieved an international corporate profile on a par with companies like Coca-Cola. The dark, bitter beer which had established the company's fame and fortune had a brand recognition second to none, and Guinness should have used this to expand into other segments of the alcohol market. Indeed, the company's one major foray into new product development had provided them with a fine example of the areas they should have been entering.

*The Silver Salver*, p.211.

The Gentlemen Make Way for the Players

## The Changing World of Beer

To the amazement and amusement of virtually every country in the western world, warm, flat beer has been Britain's most popular alcoholic drink since the Industrial Revolution. Yet from the early 1960s onwards, there was a gentle wind of change blowing through the British beer market. The Guinness board had been amongst the first people in the British brewing industry to feel this slight stirring, and they somewhat reluctantly introduced a new product to cater for what they considered would be a small but profitable market segment. Thus was born Harp lager.

This pale, sharp, gassy liquid, the complete antithesis to Guinness stout, was introduced on a trial basis in Ireland. It did remarkably well and on the strength of this test marketing it was extended to Scotland and England. Its only real competitor was Bass's Carling Black Label and it soon became brand leader in a rapidly expanding market.* The success of Harp lager should have provided the company with an object lesson in strategic marketing. Unfortunately, it did not: the company made little effort to expand into other sectors of the alcohol market, thereby missing a golden opportunity to arrest Guinness' decline before it ever really began.

The second factor that would have been obvious to the board, had they but looked hard enough, was the increasing importance of distribution and retailing—the task of actually getting their products in front of the consumer. Admittedly, Guinness were acutely conscious of their own lack of tied public houses (there were and are only three Guinness pubs, all in Ireland) which put them in a potentially very dangerous situation. In effect, the company was dependent on the good will of breweries with a large number of retail outlets. These breweries were, moreover, attempting to expand their own share of a declining market: what incentive had they to give space on the bar to a competitor's brand? There are many unenviable situations in which a company can find itself—relying on the tender mercies of its rivals to distribute its flagship brand is probably the least enviable. Whilst Guinness understood this only too well in relation to their own immediate priorities, they could not extend the principle to other areas. The company had enormous resources in the early 1960s

*In 1986, Harp lager had approximately 4.5% of the overall British beer market: Guinness stout had 1.7%.

15

and they should have been employed far more effectively than they were.

Bearing these two points in mind, and neither was beyond the wit of Guinness executives to discover, any diversification strategy adopted by the company should have been underpinned by the creation of a solid and extensive base in the brewing and distilling industries, complemented by a movement into the retail sector of the economy. Instead, the company diversified into areas as far apart as chemicals and confectionary. The only things that their acquisitions had in common was no conceivable link with the parent organisation's past expertise or future requirements. There was no consistency, no thread of internal logic, running through Guinness' diversification. When they should have been looking for companies whose products had methods of production, distribution and consumption similar to that of Guinness' major products, companies that would give the organisation a degree of synergy, they diversified in a seemingly random pattern. What, for example, did the company know of the canal boat business in France or the toothbrush market in Malaysia, neither having figured very prominently in the company's history to date? The answer was very little, yet Guinness continued to diversify into markets that were a manager's nightmare—unfamiliar products in faraway countries, about which they knew very little (to paraphrase Chamberlain).

Some commentators considered that Guinness was operating on the blunderbuss principle that if they spread their money around widely enough then they were bound to hit a target which was moving upwards. More often than not, though, the only target the company hit with any regularity was its own foot. One classic example concerned the company's attempts to break into the lucrative North American market, the largest in the world, with draught Guinness. The company had been trying to expand the tenuous foothold its stout had established in east coast cities with a large Irish-American population such as New York and Boston. However, bottled stout sold poorly, and the cost of shipping the heavy kegs of draught stout across the Atlantic made its price prohibitive. Guinness developed a special bottled brew which could be placed in a machine and bombarded with soundwaves to produce the characteristic thick, creamy Guinness head. It was not a resounding success.

Perhaps the rationale—if such it can be called—behind the company's strategy was the same as that which guided the investment of the various family trust fund monies; if so, the Guinness board were guilty of confusing corporate management decisions with personal investment criteria. In any event, by 1981 the Guinness board faced a desperate situation: they had to decide whether they were content to run the company with the structures and management philosophies that had been made obsolete by the passage of time and Britain's decline into genteel economic shabbiness, or were they to initiate a radical strategic re-orientation? They were to choose the latter.

## The Players Open their Innings

The customary calm and reserve of Ernest Saunders, vice president of the Nutritional Division of the giant Nestlé, was imperceptibly ruffled when he received a letter from Lord Iveagh inviting him to become chief executive of Guinness. He was no stranger to headhunting, having been both practitioner and victim himself in the past, but even he was a little flattered and bemused by this particular approach. On balance, however, he should not have been; his career to date and his undoubted ability, skills and energy marked him down as a marketing man of, if not pure, then near, genius. His day had finally come.

Despite his having been thrust into the unforgiving light of public scrutiny—or perhaps because of it—Ernest Walter Saunders was and still is an intensely private man. There is nothing in his appearance or manner that differentiates him from any other City businessman, save for a shrewd, intelligent gaze that suggests a first-rate business brain behind his eyes. His features and bearing have drawn the inevitable comparisons with a Roman senator, and it is a comparison too tempting to resist. One can too easily picture him as a comforting presence under a Nero or Caligula, defining his objectives, formulating his strategies and then executing them with a crispness that cuts through the chaos around him. *The Times*, discarded the Roman clichés in comparing him to the most famous product of the company he was to take over: 'His air is so unruffled as to often appear aloof. He might even be likened to a pint of Guinness, his near white hair crowning an invariably dark, sober suit. And when he speaks it is with a voice smoothly reminiscent of the famous Irish stout.' They might also have mentioned that, like the famous Irish stout, he appeared to have the ability to keep his head to the bitter end.

If Saunders' appearance invariably draws comparisons with an ancient Roman, his reticence about his private life makes him laconic to a degree that would impress the Spartans. His *Who's Who* entry says that he was born on 21st October 1935, but it does not say where, nor identify his parents. He was, in fact, born as Ernst Schleyer in Vienna and it was only in 1954—when he had already been a naturalised British subject for some time—that he changed his name by deed poll from Schleyer to Saunders. It is a measure of how successful Saunders has been in keeping his private life just that, that *Private Eye*—usually able to dig up some mud to throw around—was reduced to trying to read some significance into Saunders' change of name. This fact, allied to Saunders' Austrian origins, led Lord Gnome's organ to conclude that Saunders suffered from 'Waldheim's Disease'—an inability to recall where you were or what you did between 1937 and 1945.

In fact, Saunders has never made any effort to deny his background. It is rather that he has kept the family closet securely closed.

The beginnings of the anglicisation of young Ernst Schleyer can be traced back to a day in 1938 when Emanuel Schleyer, a prominent Jewish gynaecologist, fled Vienna with his wife Johanna and two young sons, and took up residence in the quiet London suburb of St John's Wood, at a house previously purchased by Johanna's merchant father. The new abode of the Schleyer family was at 27 Acacia Road— an address so redolent of English suburbia that it was almost a caricature. This was a good omen, perhaps, to a family which had escaped the Nazi atrocities only weeks before the regime reached Vienna, and who now hoped to forge for themselves a new life in Britain.

Although Emanuel and Johanna, by shrewd planning and timely action, had escaped their certain fate at the hand of persecutors, they did not entirely sever their links with the past. Johanna in particular held on to memories of the lavish life-style, fashionable and influential friends, and luxurious home she had left behind in Vienna. Some dearly loved pieces of antique furniture had been sent over in advance to the new house, and these were cherished as relics of a by-gone age, but Johanna never really recovered from the gross disuption of the life she loved, and there are some who maintain that she never lost hope that one day they would return. An old friend, Frau Louise Kirnig, now 79 but still living in a flat below the old Schleyer apartment, remembers: 'Frau Schleyer asked me to look after the apartment, you know, open the window now and again. In return she gave me some money and furniture. I think she really believed she would come back here one day'.*

On the face of it, Emanuel adjusted more readily to his new, albeit reduced, circumstances. He quickly became fluent in English, so that he was able to re-qualify in his profession and continue to practise. He never quite let go of his Austrian connections, however, even after taking Saunders as the new family name, he also held on to the old one, calling himself Schleyer-Saunders.

While the family began to carve a niche for themselves in an adopted country, the old Schleyer apartment, which had so lately rung with the voices of elevated members of society enjoying lavish hospitality, now became accustomed to new sounds: the stomping of boots and the brusque issue of military orders, as the officers of the *Wehrmacht* moved in.

If the parents of Ernest Saunders retained an affectionate nostalgia for the place which had once been their home, he himself does not appear to have been influenced by it. His decision to ignore, if not deny, his past is difficult to explain, although Geoffrey Levy, writing for the *Daily Mail*, made an admirable attempt: 'It was an experience . . . that understandably influenced his whole life, manifesting itself in two characteristics. One, an overwhelming need to run faster and achieve more than anyone else, almost to compensate for his family's humiliation and loss in the thirties. And, two, an overriding need to assimilate himself into his new country, to hide both his Jewish faith and past, the very things which had raised the death of so many of his family's Viennese friends at the hands of the Nazis.'†

Nevertheless, there is nothing particularly ignominious in the story of the Schleyers' flight from persecution.

At the age of nine, Saunders was enrolled at Caldicot preparatory school, near Windsor, as Ernest Schleyer. It may well have been here that he encountered the anti-German feeling which was running so high at that time, particularly among schoolboys, who will embrace any cause which gives them an excuse to taunt their fellows. As anyone who has ever been a schoolboy—but perhaps particularly at a private preparatory school—will admit, altruism is not a strong point with the

*Daily Mail*, 23rd January 1987
†*Daily Mail*, 23rd January 1987

young. In the absence of any other weakness, such as red hair or a stammer, with which to tease a schoolmate, an unusual name can be a perfectly good excuse, and a foreign name which sounds very much as if it has links with one's own country's greatest enemy would provide unlimited scope for the cruelty which a juvenile mind can devise. Young Ernst Schleyer may have suffered more than he cares to admit. Certainly, when he progressed to St. Paul's four years later, he preferred to be known as Saunders.

If the man volunteers little to connect him with his Viennese background, then he offers even less to connect him with the Jewish faith. In all things, Saunders wishes to be seen as the archetypal Englishman, including regular attendance at his local church. The vicar, Oscar Muspratt, had no idea that Saunders was not a Christian by birth, and does not know whether or not he has formally converted, but he expects to see Mr Saunders in his congregation about once a month, and his wife, Carole, is a stalwart of the church: a member of the Church Ladies Committee, a popular woman in the parish, and even a darner of the vicar's socks.

Carole Saunders is, by all accounts, a likeable and vivacious woman, strongly supportive of her husband and possessed of such good sense that she is often supposed to be used as a sounding board for her husband's business decisions.

It is curious, then, that here is another notable omission from the Ernest Saunders entry in *Who's Who*. The names of his wife's parents, usually included as a courtesy, are absent.

The picture becomes clearer when one discovers that Carole's parents, Henry and Maureen Stephings, have not been on speaking terms with their son-in-law for almost 25 years: since before their daughter's marriage to Saunders at St. John's Church in Hampstead in 1963. Saunders met his wife-to-be at a London party, when she was a 19 year-old secretary at the Bank of England. The cause of the blazing row which took place around that time between Saunders and Carole's father is shrouded in mystery. Maureen Stephings claims that the subject is too painful to discuss, and there is certainly no love lost between Saunders and Henry Stephings. 'I hear that my daughter's husband is the most hated man in London', he said in an interview with the *Daily Mail*. 'I'm not surprised'.*

What lies behind those words is a matter for conjecture. Certainly

*Daily Mail*, 23rd January 1987

there are many who will testify to Saunders' skills at marketing products, but testimonials to his personal attributes are thinner on the ground. His rise through the ranks of his profession is easier to document than his fiercely protected private life. So just where did Ernest Saunders the marketing man come from?

Saunders came down from Emanuel College, Cambridge in 1959 with a Class 2:II degree in Law (i.e. a mediocre degree—the brilliant either get 'firsts'—because that is what they should get or 'thirds' because they do no work or because they are too clever for the examiners to understand them!). His sharp intellect, powerful analytical skills and imposing physical presence would undoubtedly have assured him a comfortable living at the Bar or with a firm of City solicitors, but he chose not to practise law. Instead, he preferred to begin a career in marketing at J. Walter Thompson, then the world's largest advertising agency.*

Saunders stayed with J. Walter Thompson for over five years, familiarising himself with the theory and practice of the marketing ethos then just beginning to permeate the thinking of British management. In 1965 he left the agency to work for the multi-national pharmaceutical group Beecham. He left there in 1973 to become chairman of the European division of the mail-order company Great Universal Stores, a position worthy of his obvious talents and ambition. Four years later he moved again, this time to Geneva and a top position with the giant Nestlé Group. It was with Nestlé that he was to have his first major involvement in a controversy.

## Other Players Come in

From the mid 1970s onwards, the nutritional division of Nestlé, concerned at the falling sales of its baby foods and powdered milk products in Europe and the United States, embarked on a vigorous campaign to expand their market in the Third World. Some people,

---

*Ironically enough, it was during his time at J. Walter Thompson that Saunders first came into contact with the company he was to run over two decades later. The agency was then handling the highly prestigious and lucrative Guinness account, and they had good reason to recall their former employee with something less than paternalistic pride and fondness when, shortly after his appointment as chief executive in 1981, he placed Guinness advertising with another agency.

however, thought the campaign went beyond the bounds of legitimate marketing aggression.

The main thrust of the Nestlé campaign was to persuade—or 're-educate'—nursing mothers in the underdeveloped world that the use of milk powder in solution with water was preferable to breast feeding their infants. This in itself was nothing less than a lie: powdered milk is, nutritionally speaking, far inferior to breast feeding and furthermore lactation in women also acts as a powerful natural contraceptive, a factor of some significance in the over-populated Third World. In their search to create and penetrate new markets, Nestlé were guilty of showing more than just the unacceptable face of capitalism. By bringing the full weight of their not inconsiderable marketing expertise to bear on the ignorant, unsophisticated women of Africa, Asia and Central and South America, Nestlé proved to many that the key to running a successful multi-national was to fob off on uninformed consumers products they did not need at prices they could not afford. What turned the controversy into nothing less than an international scandal was the fact that the milk powder was, in many cases, being reconstituted with contaminated water.

The company came under intense pressure from a coalition of groups in 35 countries called the 'Baby Food Action Network'. The major weapon in the Network's armoury was the very real threat of a consumer boycott of Nestlé products in the United States. The exact nature of Saunders' role in the baby milk scandal remains unclear: he certainly cannot be blamed for initiating the entry into—or rather the creation of—a Third World market, as this began before Saunders was a Nestlé employee. Understandably, neither Saunders nor his one-time Swiss employers are eager to reopen the episode.

What is clear, however, is the cynical, almost Machiavellian way he went about extricating Nestlé from the scandal. What is also clear is that it was in this protection of Nestlé that Saunders forged relationships with the Swiss Artur Furer and the American Thomas Ward, key figures in the 1986 dramas at Guinness. By 1980, Saunders was vice president of Nestlé's nutritional division, and he had as his first priority (as a confidential memorandum from him to Artur Furer, then Nestlé's General Manager, put it) 'third party rebuttals of the activists case'—which was to say the dissemination of little more than propaganda via some unsuspecting third party. The medium chosen for such a manoeuvre was a right wing American foundation, the Ethics and Public Policy Centre, with which Saunders maintained close links through Thomas Ward, Nestlé's representative in Washington.

In September 1979 the president of the Ethics and Public Policy Centre, Ernest Lefever, had paid *Fortune* magazine journalist Herman Nickel US$5,000 to study the baby milk issue. The study was due around February 1980, during which month Nestlé donated US$5,000 to the foundation's general fund. The study finally appeared in the form of an article in the June issue of *Fortune*, and Nestlé was highly pleased with its overall tone and conclusions. Perhaps its most memorable phrase was 'Marxists marching under the banner of Christ'. Saunders' memorandum to Furer spoke of 'the tremendous opportunities at last provided by the *Fortune* magazine,' and the Nestlé public relations machine moved into gear. At the same time, Nestlé donated another US$20,000 to the foundation's general fund.

Thomas Ward met Lefever in Washington, and it was agreed that the foundation would reprint the article for general release. This was duly done, and the reprints were sent out on a mailing list obtained from Nestlé's public relations firm. The cost of this mail shot was a further US$10,000 and—'by pure coincidence' according to Lefever—Ward gave the centre another US$10,000. The only man to emerge with his integrity unscathed by this rather shoddy affair was the journalist Herman Nickel (who later became US ambassador to South Africa). When he heard of Nestlé's involvement in the project he stopped work on the study at once. He was never paid.

## Like a Wolf on the Fold

The inducement of an annual salary of £110,000 and the challenge of reviving what was described as 'one of the dullest companies on the scene' was still not inducement enough for Ernest Saunders to accept the Earl of Iveagh's offer at once. He discussed it for several weeks with his wife, Carole, and mulled it over in his own mind on the long, solitary walks it was his habit to take. Ultimately, however, the challenge proved irresistible; Ernest Saunders became chief executive of one of Britain's most genteel business institutions.

Saunders came down on Guinness like a wolf on the fold. One former employee recalls his first brush with the man charged with taking the company into the nineties: 'Not to put too fine a point on it—and Ernest Saunders certainly didn't—he came, he saw, and he kicked ass! We had never seen anything like it. He had a phenomenal grasp of detail, and could ask you the most awkward questions—to which he invariably knew the answers. After the first five minutes of meeting him, you knew that things were going to change and change fast.'

It probably took Saunders less than five minutes to reach the same conclusion. Looking back on the purges of his first two years, Saunders remarked, 'Guinness had been badly managed for 100 years. We had one product, a follow-the-flag British Empire earnings base, and a management of production orientated people.'

The first six months of Saunders' reign were spent cutting his way through the tangle of nearly 300 companies that were the fruits of Guinness' diversification, trying to isolate current and potential profit centres. His gut feeling was that very few such profitable businesses existed within the company's portfolio. Over 6,000 man-hours of research and analysis later, his feelings were confirmed and he knew that his first objective was to trim Guinness down to more manageable proportions.

In the next two years Saunders was to preside over one of the largest exercises in divestment undertaken by a British company. During this period he sold off or closed down 140 Guinness-owned companies, retaining a central core of retailing interests with Lavells the newsagents, Drummonds the chemists, and Clares the shopfitting business. It was a decidedly expensive catharsis, and one which tested the nerve of the Guinness board; in the company accounts for 1982, £49 million was written off as exceptional items.

However, Saunders saw it as a necessary evil, and was convinced that the ends would provide ample justification of his means: 'I wanted to give myself a platform to build a big branded business, he said. I regard investments in brands in the same way as others regard capital investment.'

With the shedding of Guinness' more meaningless holdings, Saunders had implemented the first part of his grand strategy. It was, essentially, a defensive action aimed at staunching the flow of resources out of the company. The second, offensive, element of the strategy was to change the management orientation of the company and 'go into the 1990s making good profits'.

To effect this, however, required more than just the determination of the chief executive. Before Saunders could embark on any meaningful structural change he needed a cadre of top level managers, steeped in marketing ethos, on whom he could rely. Speaking afterwards, he summed up his attitude: 'Anyone who puts me in charge of running a business knows by now what they are going to get; a revitalisation done in the most constructive way—but probably with some pain'.

There was pain a-plenty; one of his victims remembers: 'He went through us like a dose of salts. He didn't like much about our current set-up. And to a point you had to agree with him. Guinness really did have too many people who had risen beyond the levels of their own incompetence. For example, we had dozens of accountants running around the place, yet he couldn't lay his hands on a coherent set of accounts. And the marketing department thought it had been hard at it if they spent half a day looking at the latest copy from J. Walter Thompson. Saunders went in spouting all this stuff he'd picked up at Nestlé or wherever, and most of them looked at him as if he was speaking double Dutch.'

The new chief executive used whatever weapons he had in his considerable armoury to get what he wanted: flattery, cajolery, promises, threats and on occasion downright bullying. It soon became obvious to all concerned that he did not suffer fools gladly: 'He had a way of looking at you—or maybe through you—that said quite clearly "You are nothing but an insignificant little man." The thing was, after you'd been on the end of it a couple of times you began to believe that you *were* an insignificant little man.'

Undoubtedly, Saunders made enemies during his early days at Guinness. He also won the admiration of many and inspired a fierce loyalty among his staff: 'I have no idea where the nickname "Deadly" Ernest came from, it just appeared one day. But we used it in a grudgingly affectionate way; of course he was shaking us up, because that was what he was paid to do. You had to admire the guy, for his energy, for his vision, I suppose. He had a tremendous charisma, and we began to get a sense of purpose, we were going places. After a while morale was pretty good.'

## The Bainies

Not even Saunders' energy and ability could mould Guinness' upper management into the shape he wanted. Instead, he was forced to return to the organisations that had honed his own native talents to a fine edge; Artur Furer was brought in from Nestlé, and Saunders scoured the files of consultancies to find the right man to mastermind a financial strategy. It did not take him long to decide on Olivier Roux, a high-flier with Bain and Co.

In the world of management consultancy, where a company's success is measured by how prestigious its list of clients is, Bain and Co. are so discreet as to draw attention to themselves. The organisation has very little to say about itself and even less about its clients, to the point of not only refusing to say what they are doing but also refusing to say for whom they are doing it. This stems less from old world courtesy and more from the hyper-competitive philosophy of the company's chairman, William Bain, who says, 'You have to be paranoid about competitors. You don't just analyse them, you see a threat in everything they do. You must overestimate their strengths and over-react to their challenges.'

Bain and Saunders spoke a common language. William Bain had also shown that he could practise what he preached. Bain and Co. was established when he and four fellow executives left the Boston Consulting Group in 1973 to set up on their own. In less than a decade, they had built the company up into the second biggest consultancy in the world, with offices in Boston, San Francisco, Munich, Paris, Tokyo and London. Their staff of professional consultants numbered 600, and these 'Bainies' were estimated to generate the company up to £1 million a month in revenue. Those companies who had used Bain consultants to help them annihilate their competitors would say that they earned every penny of it. Saunders certainly thought so and the recent court case in Jersey revealed that Bain and Co. had been paid fees of £17.5 million by Guinness.

Bain seemed unworried by descriptions of Bain and Co. as 'the Moonies of the management consulting business', 'the KGB of the industry', and 'the firm where machismo is second only to secretiveness'. In fact such comments all helped the mystique.

Bain and Co. built its success by cashing in on the dissatisfaction felt by some large corporations with the approach of many consultants who appeared to walk in, tell the client their problems, pick up a fat fee, and walk out again. Bain and Co. expressed itself uninterested in project work; they wanted to be involved right from the beginning in the corporation's strategic planning.

Its presentations to clients are of a very high calibre though its supposed unwillingness to enter into a competitive situation with other consultancies is a myth. The company also concentrates on becoming close to the chief executive. If you have his ear and everyone in the company knows it, that makes you much more effective. This closeness to the chief executive is also important if you send in several consultants and at Guinness there were up to 50 'Bainies'.

In the two years Saunders had been at Guinness he had worked what many people considered to be a miracle. The changes he had wrought in the company reached from the very top to the very bottom. He had cast his eye over every aspect of the company's structure and left little untouched. This had even extended to its advertising, hitherto Guinness' pride and joy. The old 'ad-man' in Saunders had detected a central dichotomy in Guinness' promotional activities: he considered that in the past Guinness advertising had been so powerful that it had become divorced from the product it was supposed to sell; 'One almost felt there was a second product: there was Guinness beer and then there was Guinness advertising'.

## The New Marketeers

With a notable lack of sentimentality, Saunders took the Guinness account away from his first employers, J. Walter Thompson, and placed it with the younger, less genteel Allen Brady and Marsh.* The new agency produced the amusing 'Guinnless' promotional campaign which continued the tradition of enjoyable Guinness advertising, but had only a limited and temporary effect on sales. They lost the prestigious account after two years, but not before Ernest Saunders had enjoyed, if that is the right word, some exciting moments with that great showman of the advertising world, Peter Marsh.

Saunders has always had a habit of being friendly with people while they are helping him and then cutting them off when he perceives that they are no longer of any use. Usually there is no row, he just becomes unavailable. Most people find it odd, even hurtful, but shrug their shoulders and get on with life. Some, however, do not like 'I'm sorry, Mr Saunders is unavailable'.

Peter Marsh has not helped to build one of the country's foremost advertising agencies by being diverted with 'I'm sorry, Mr Saunders

---

*In fairness J. Walter Thompson had been guilty of a certain complacent profligacy as far as Guinness were concerned. In 1979, they announced that the new Guinness campaign would resurrect the famous toucan of the 1950s. The agency spent £3,000 of Guinness' money building a radio controlled model of a toucan, which proved unworkable. Finally, they settled for a live toucan for a daily fee of £75 'plus expenses'.

is unavailable' and he marched round to the Guinness offices early one morning in 1982 when they were still in Albemarle Street and presented himself. He received the by now customary, 'I'm sorry, Mr Saunders is unavailable' to which he replied, 'That's OK, I'll wait'. And wait he did, nearly all day, with two square boxes he had brought with him. Eventually he could be ignored no longer and he was shown into Saunders' office. March opened one of his boxes, took out a First

World War German helmet and put it on Saunders' head. He then opened the other box, took out a First World War British helmet, placed it on his own head and said: 'Now Ernest, you've been in the bloody trenches for the last few weeks. Let's come out and sort out our problems'. In fact Saunders should have been getting used to Marsh's outrageous behaviour as he had enjoyed previous Marsh extravaganza at his own house in Penn, Buckinghamshire, always referred to in the popular press as a mansion.

In the summer of 1982 Saunders gave a fortieth birthday party for his wife Carole with 200 guests and a marquee on the lawn with a string quartet in the corner. It was a lovely day and with all the guests assembled in the garden a helicopter swooped down and showered them all with rose petals. The helicopter then landed and out stepped Peter Marsh dressed in a white silk suit, white shirt, white tie and bright yellow Wellington boots. We can be sure that Saunders loved being up-staged by that!

In these early days at Guinness while Saunders was getting to grips with the problems of the company his work rate was prodigious. A Guinness consultant from these early days can remember business meetings at 7.30 a.m. and can remember the enormous drive, enormous energy and tremendous ambition. He was not so sure about the financial ability and noted that Saunders did not seem to know what PE ratios were. He thought that was strange for the chief executive of a large public company.

The Guinness family, however, were delighted with their new chief executive, who they considered had single-handedly preserved the base on which their fortunes depended. As Ivan Fallon of the *Sunday Times* reported: 'They regarded him in much the same light as they looked on the man who ran the family estates or the head gamekeeper—he was the hired professional who ran the family business.*

From everyone's point of view he had run that business exceedingly well. Profits had increased by 240 per cent, the return on capital had risen from 16 per cent to 21 per cent, and the share price had experienced a sevenfold increase. But this was merely the fruits of a strategy of rationalisation; Saunders knew that the company had to grow, and the hard fact was that beer was a market in decline. No amount of advertising or skilful marketing could do anything more than alter market share in a shrinking market. Expansion could only come about through diversification, but this time it would be diversification guided by a central logic into areas with which Guinness were familiar, alcohol and retailing.

Between June 1984 and August 1985, Guinness embarked on a £121 million spending spree which, in those pre-Bell's and Distillers days, many considered to be audacious. It began with the £46 million takeover of Martin's the national confectionery, newspaper and tobacconist chain. It was followed in November by the acquisition of the up-market health resort, Champney's, at a cost of £3 million.† In January of 1985 Nature's Best Health was acquired for £2 million.

*Sunday Times*, 11th January 1987

†There is a touching story attached to the acquisition of Champney's. It was reported that Carole Saunders had spent a week there, and her husband was so impressed with the results that he bought it. Shades of Victor Kayam! It is touching, but probably apocryphal: Saunders looked at Champney's books, looked at market trends, and acquired a sound investment, which he expanded with his next purchase, Nature's Best Health.

Richter Brothers, the delicatessen chain, at £18 million, and the 7-Eleven franchise for neighbourhood stores at £16 million came in February. June saw the purchase of Lewis Meeson, the main operating company in the Barker and Dobson retail group, for nearly £10 million. This deal came only three months after Lewis Meeson had announced a pre-tax loss of £2 million during 1984, blamed on a 'lack of management control'. As such, it was an irresistible target for Saunders.

In the same week that Guinness acquired Lewis Meeson, it announced a record first-half profit of £37 million. Much of this improvement came from its expanding non-brewing activities, and retailing now accounted for about 22 per cent of the group's results. Some financial journalists were already beginning to speak of Guinness as the 'brewing and retail giant'. It was the first time in years that that description had not been prefaced with 'troubled'.

Saunders' activities may have been beginning to bring him to the notice of Fleet Street and to the bosom of the Guinness family, but as far as he was concerned the expansion of the company had only raised it to a 'Sunday league' status. He had his sights set firmly on Division I. This could not be done without a quantum leap, an action or series of actions which would propel Guinness into the major league and make the £100 million plus spending of the past year look insignificant.

After establishing a healthy retailing base, Saunders now had to capitalise on Guinness' expertise in brewing to expand their stake in the world's alcoholic drinks market. His research had shown quite clearly that on current trends the international scene was likely to become the preserve of a handful of conglomerates by the 1990s. The most awesome threat was posed by the Japanese distilling group Suntory. The American Anheuser-Busch, with its Budweiser brand, was making rapid advances, and the two Canadian firms of Seagrams and Hiram Walker were not far behind. Finally, there was the maverick Australian John Elliot, with his Elders-IXL combine and his desire for a major international coup (later materialising in his unsuccessful £2 billion bid for Allied Lyons). Saunders recalls his feelings: 'A lot of people will tell you they are a worldwide business. They mean they have one bottle of their drink somewhere in every country. That does not mean worldwide. In bars, at events, parties, in aeroplanes you are subjected to brand names. The same groups seemed to be appearing all over the place. We decided that to become a major player we had to make a major move.' The major move was to be the takeover of Arthur Bell and Co.

# THREE

## The Battle for Bell's

### A Reconnaissance in Depth

If there was one single factor that characterised Ernest Saunders'
approach to any given problem then it was his thoroughness. Allied to
his native managerial talent and his highly analytical mind was an
enormous capacity for hard work, which gave him not only an
understanding of the overall situation but also a grasp of fine detail and
minutiae which made him more than a match for those who were to
become his adversaries. He had demonstrated this ability since his
earliest days at J. Walter Thompson; it had carried him to the top in the
marketing sections of major multi-nationals, and now it was going to
be employed in his campaign to capture Arthur Bell and Co. for
Guinness and lay the foundations of an international trading empire.

31

Saunders was also intelligent enough to realise his own limitations. He was the delegator *par excellence*, employing teams of professionals in areas about which he knew very little. One such area was the Scottish business scene, the economic land behind the tartan curtain, whose customs, traditions and mores made it a potential minefield for any brash southerner chancing his arm. Guinness' chief executive needed what amounted to a mentor, someone who would be willing and able to give him some direction through the *terra incognita* of Scotland. All the advice Saunders could obtain pointed to one man, Charles Annand Fraser.

'Impeccable' always seems like an understatement when applied to Charles Fraser, almost as if the praise is too faint. His 20 or so directorships in Great Britain and the USA include United Biscuits and Scottish television. His highly astute business mind and great charm have brought him success and the chance for his legal firm, W. and J. Burness to play the key marketing role. But that is only one facet of the man. His *Who's Who* entry reveals that along with the traditional executive pastimes of ski-ing and squash he indulges in that most incomprehensively Scottish of pleasures, piping. He also glories in the title of Purse Bearer to the Lord High Commissioner to the General Assembly of the Church of Scotland, which translates as the Queen's representative in Scotland.

Fraser is the type of man to take his duties seriously; he is also the type of man to take the contacts his various positions give him seriously as well. His reputation as a man who gets things done was already well established in England. When Eddy Shah, seeking funds for the launch of *Today* was rebuffed by the sceptical money men of the City, it was Charles Fraser who mediated between Shah and the even more cautious—yet perhaps more imaginative—fund managers in Edinburgh. It was this type of ability and the reputation Fraser enjoyed in Europe's second largest money market which led Saunders to his door.

One of the most important pieces of background information Fraser was able to give Saunders concerned the standing, or rather lack of it, which Raymond Miquel, the chairman of Bell's since 1973, enjoyed in the eyes of the Scottish business establishment. Putting it bluntly, Miquel was not popular; if Saunders went about his task carefully, then few of the Scottish institutions would shed many tears over the demise of Miquel.

An ageing Tory member for the shires once told Julian Critchley, then a young MP, that the Conservative Party seemed to have lost a button off its cuff. He meant that the new intake of Tory MPs lacked a certain breeding. The Scottish establishment, looking at Raymond Miquel, might equally remark that he sought to remove the very sleeve. The grandees of the Scottish scene might sniff and say of some that they were not quite pukka; no such niceties were reserved for Miquel—he was merely an upstart, a parvenu, a 'flash harry'. In truth, and notwithstanding his undoubted business acumen, Miquel lacked either the background or the charm to gain any real social acceptance in Scotland. He had been born in Glasgow to a Scottish mother and French father who worked as a chef. Whilst such humble antecedents may have been socially acceptable if they were left safely behind in the eighteenth century—as were the Guinness's—they are likely to prove something of a disadvantage if they were only recently deceased.

Whether Miquel courted such snobbery by way of his *arriviste* behaviour, or whether his behaviour was the natural reaction to the snobbery of which he felt himself to be the victim, is a moot point: what is clear, however, is that he was a very capable manager who had risen almost from the shopfloor. He had spent all his working life at Bell's, joining them in 1956 as a works study engineer. He became production controller in 1958, and director in 1962. Another six years saw his elevation to managing director, and by 1973 he had become chairman of the company. His rise had been the result of sheer hard work and a dynamic, driving style of 'hands-on' management.* If Bell's had been good for Miquel, then he had been good for Bell's. However, as the company entered the 1980s some observers were expressing their concern as to Miquel's suitability to remain at the helm of Bell's. One insider remarked, 'He did a superb job, especially when Bell's was a small company and he could run it himself. But as it got bigger he became less comfortable. It got too big for him'.

This presents an interesting parallel with Ernest Saunders, the man with whom Miquel was soon to come into rancorous conflict. Both men were effectively workaholics, both men expected and obtained the maximum from their lieutenants, and both men were almost obsessive about overseeing the tiniest details of their respective strategies. On two counts, though, Saunders was in a different league from Miquel.

---

*Miquel's desire to inculcate a strong team spirit amongst his workforce took on a half-legendary, half-comical aspect. At official receptions, he and his sales team would be clad in identical green blazers; and every year, during a sales briefing weekend, there would be a compulsory sports day for sales staff.

First he had what might be called a 'global' vision and a clarity of thought which enabled him to operate the largest of companies with a singularity of purpose. And on a tactical level he knew precisely when, and more importantly to whom, he should delegate the planning and supervision of a particular operation. Saunders was the modern professional manager, and as such had the utmost faith in his fellow professionals and the techniques they had at their disposal. Miquel, like so many gifted men who came up the hard way, could never quite accept that some things were best left to subordinates. As a consequence, he had begun to spread himself too thinly. His energies and talents had effected a remarkable turnaround in Bell's flagging fortunes in his early days as chairman; pre-tax profits had grown from £3.02 million in 1974 to £35.17 million in 1984 when Bell's whisky had secured 21 per cent of the domestic market and in 1982 had captured an astonishing 25 per cent. But the environment was changing and there were doubts as to whether Miquel, with his distinctive style of leadership, could change with it.

Even at what might be seen as the peak of Miquel's success there were signs that structural changes within the whisky industry had rubbed some of the lustre from Bell's performance. The Scottish whisky industry as a whole had entered the 1980s faced with falling demand, heavy overstocking and the spectre of closures and liquidations confronting it. Bell's looked set to weather the storm better than most, but there was certainly no room for complacency at the company's Cherrybank headquarters in Perth. Probably the greatest threat lay in the overall decline of the Scotch whisky market. The consumer profile for whisky was beginning to look very old; the white spirits—vodka, gin and white rum—were more attractive to the young, and the growth in the consumption of wine and even non-alcoholic drinks had all taken their toll. The Perrier generation had arrived, to the ultimate detriment of one of Scotland's major industries.

By 1984, Bell's premium blend whisky, which accounted for 92 per cent of all its whisky sales, was facing increased pressure from both cut-price blends and supermarket own-labels at one end of the market, and from Highland Distilleries' Famous Grouse at the other. Bell's still maintained 21 per cent of the home market, compared with Grouse's 9.4 per cent, but this represented a 4 per cent fall from the heady days of 1982, when the company accounted for just over a quarter of all the whisky sold in Britain. Nor did the picture overseas give any cause for unrestrained optimism. Bell's exported to some 130 countries around the world, and between 1974 and 1984 turnover had risen from £6.7 million to £38.6 million. However, with the exception of South Africa, the company had no brand leader in any of these markets. This was painfully obvious in the United States.

America was, of course, the key market for any distiller and invariably the most difficult to penetrate. Yet Bell's should have enjoyed a far better fate in the USA than it did. Americans had a fondness for Scotch whisky dating back to the 1940s, when the spirit was nothing less than liquid gold used to redress Britain's trade imbalance with the 'arsenal of democracy'. American servicemen stationed in Great Britain—virtually the only people who could afford the luxury of whisky in those lean times—soon grew to prefer it to their own bourbons and ryes. Given that Bell's had a premium product aimed at a highly receptive market, they should certainly have made far greater inroads than they did. Their downfall lay in their distribution strategy: the company was notoriously unfortunate in its choice of agents, and it was only in 1984, when Miquel acquired the American firm of Wellington Importers, that Bell's established the distribution network which might make for the most effective marketing of Bell's whisky in the US. By 1985, however, the company was still only selling a nominal 50,000 cases a year there. This inability to penetrate the American market was to become one of the main weapons in Saunders' attack on Bell's.

Like Guinness, Arthur Bell and Co. was also conscious of the vulnerability of a single product base. And like Guinness, their response was diversification: however, Bell's stayed largely to what it knew best, the production, bottling and distribution of premium whisky. In 1984, for example, Miquel circumvented the then shortage of glass by acquiring Canning Town Glass Co. The company was running at a substantial loss when Bell's purchased it, and even after major investment and rationalisation it was still considered to be something of a disappointment.

Diversification did not stop with the ill-starred London Glass Co. In January 1984, Miquel made a move for the Gleneagles Hotel Group, with an initial offer of £20 million. Gleneagles Hotels had been set up in 1981 to buy the two notable Edinburgh hotels, the Caledonian and the North British, and the Gleneagles itself in Perthshire. All three had previously been owned by British Rail, which had never quite got there as far as hotel management was concerned:

despite their international reputation, the three hotels had managed to make a £12,000 loss in their last year under British Rail. The Gleneagles Hotel Group was set up by the British Linen Bank who cast around for a management team worthy of the venture's potential. To head the team they chose 37-year-old Peter Tyrie, poached from Ramada Hotels International. Over £10 million was spent on refurbishing the properties, and within a year the Group was realising its £500,000 profit target. There were plans to progress through the Unlisted Securities Market towards a full stock market listing. It was not to be, however. In an attempt to enter the lucrative London market, the Group acquired the Piccadilly Hotel in London. Tyrie had examined the venture, and considered that a London base was essential to tap in on the influx of American tourists. Ostensibly, the Piccadilly Hotel seemed ideal: it was plush, prestigious, and had the right image. In his haste, however, Tyrie overlooked the fact that it was also confined to a very small site with no room for expansion and refurbishment—two things which it desperately needed.

Somewhere close to £10 million was needed to buy and refurbish the Piccadilly, and Tyrie approached St Martin's Property to finance the deal. It was at this point that several members of the Gleneagles board threatened to mutiny. They were unhappy about a proposed £9.7 million rights issue, and the arrangements made with St Martin's. But before a full blown split could develop, Miquel stepped in. The resulting takeover battle was acrimonious, and with hindsight some considered it to be a foretaste of the later Guinness/Bell's clash. By February, Bell's had been forced to raise its bid from £20 million to £27 million: the increase was sufficient to persuade four major institutional shareholders to accept the bid. Miquel might have thought that he had gained a major profit centre in his diversification policy; in retrospect, he may simply have sown the seeds of the defeat he was later to reap. For he had not only gained four prestigious hotels, he had also gained an expensive cash drain and Peter Tyrie as a member of the Bell's board of management. He would have reason later to regret both.

More immediately, certain aspects of the Gleneagles deal were worrying both those within and without Bell's, and some were even suggesting that Miquel was no longer the man to run the company. The Bell's board were uneasy about Miquel's commitment to refurbish the Piccadilly: major structural faults had been discovered, there were problems with contractors, and the initial estimate of £11 million ended up as a bill of £17 million. Equally worrying were the increasingly frequent trips Miquel was making to the US in his attempts to increase sales there and seek out future hotels to acquire. In March 1984, the brokers Campbell Neill, contemplating half-yearly profit figures on Bell's whisky business, were moved to advise shareholders to dispose of some of their holdings.

## The Assault

Some observers remarked that the timing of Guinness's bid for Bell's was a stroke of tactical genius on the part of Ernest Saunders. Raymond Miquel was asleep in Chicago, and the rest of the board was scattered throughout the world with some as far afield as Hong Kong. However, if genius it was then it was a genius that had been thrust upon Saunders: something, or someone, had alerted the stock market that a major move was afoot. Bell's shares had undergone two significant rises at the end of April 1985 and the middle of May and moved up sharply again in the week beginning 10th June. Guinness's bid on Friday 14th June 1985 was designed to pre-empt any further rises.

What was most astonishing about these rises was that according to Bell's recently announced half-yearly results, tactfully described as 'disappointing', they should never have occurred at all. The Bell's board had been looking to slow down the decline in their share price (which had been halved between 1983 and 1985) more than anything else.

Saunders was too subtle a strategist to insult the Bell's shareholders with a derisory initial offer. Instead, he planned to make the institutional shareholders an offer they could hardly refuse by giving them a significant profit on their holdings. However, what amounted to a magnanimous gesture when Bell's stood at 130p was laughably inadequate when they soared to 170p. Saunders was visibly shaken, and demanded a Stock Exchange inquiry (ironic when viewed from the spring of 1987).

What, then, was the cause of a rise which, on the fact of it, should never have happened? Opinions vary: Frank Malcolm of Bell's, Lawrie, Macgregor, Bell's brokers, was adamant that the rise was based on something more than mere speculation. 'The market definitely knew,' he commented at the time. 'You can tell the difference between rumour and hard fact, and somebody was acting on hard fact.'

If there was a leak, then it could only have come from a source within Guinness, as neither Bell's nor any of its advisers had been contacted prior to the bid being made public. Indeed, in an effort to allay suspicion and camouflage their intentions, Guinness had not purchased any Bell's shares prior to the announcement of the bid: unusually, then, the company had embarked on their campaign without a single Bell's share. Saunders, perhaps overestimating the loyalty which he thought he commanded amongst his 'war cabinet', gave little credence to the leak theory: 'Very few people knew anything about our plans,' he said, 'it was a very small circle. The day after the bid I asked my secretary if she had been surprised. She said yes—she'd had no idea'.

Searching around for someone to blame, Saunders' gaze fell upon the Japanese whisky producers Suntory. Mindful of the propaganda value of Guinness appearing to fight off a foreign competitor, he hinted that the Japanese company could be responsible for the rise in Bell's share price. He voiced these suspicions in a comment: 'Maybe I'm already the white knight, having seen off the yellow peril.'

However, if Saunders had been rushed into making his bid for Bell's, his careful preparation in the months preceding the July announcement were to stand him in good stead. Following Charles Fraser's advice, Saunders had built up a team with sufficient Scottish colouring to enable him to negotiate his way through the traps laid down by Scottish sentiment which could so easily catch the unwary Englishman. He had no desire to see his bid for Bell's being referred to the Monopolies Commission, as had been the case with bids for the Royal Bank of Scotland, Highland Distilleries, and Anderson Strathclyde.

Wood Mackenzie, Guinness's brokers, were not unaware of both the good and the bad points of the Scotch whisky industry. More importantly, perhaps, Saunders had enlisted the services of Scottish merchant bankers Noble Grossart who were to be given equal billing with Morgan Grenfell in the bid. In approaching Noble Grossart, Saunders had acted on advice from two notable City figures, Gerald Ronsen and ironically James Gulliver. Their counsel was eminently sound: the bank was a small Edinburgh institution which under the leadership of Angus Grossart had become well known for its impeccable 'Scottishness'. This nationalist sentiment was in many ways a reflection of the personality of the eloquent, urbane Grossart who had built the bank up into a flexible, multi-skilled organisation able to compete with all the other well known banks on an international scale. In a profile in June 1986, *Financial Weekly* summarised Grossart thus: 'In some ways the Grossart vision of the Scottish financial scene is complex and, dare one say, very Scottish; a small home base . . . a history of international exposure developed to maintain and nourish the financial skills, yet a strong nationalistic urge to denounce the evils of London . . . he can be quite scathing about what he sees as the growth of a rather dangerous "macho atmosphere in London" as far as merchant banking is concerned.'

As such, Grossart was not the sort of man to be swept off his feet by the blandishments of Saunders or the prestige which might accrue from the bid. He took several days to consider the offer and all its implications before finally reaching his decision. His acceptance of Saunders' offer was a major triumph for Guinness; it boosted the company's credibility in Scotland, and was sufficient testimony for many Scottish institutions.

Upon the announcement of the £325 million bid for Bell's the Guinness machine went smoothly into action. On Monday 17th June, Saunders flew to Glasgow to hold his first press conference: he was articulate, accessible and polite, but he never wavered from his central message that a Guinness takeover would be 'good for Bell's and good for Scotland'. He spent the remainder of the week going round the 'great' and the 'good' in Scottish life, seeing anyone who was anyone. He even managed to manifest a certain humility and impressed everybody he met with his eagerness to listen and learn, to absorb the Scottish perspective. He listened to the Scottish Whisky Association, he listened to George Younger, he listened to the Scottish Development Agency, and then he would expound his own views on the ills that beset the whisky industry and the long term threats that faced it. He spoke of the threat to the spirits market in general from the health boom, and the impact on the whisky market from white spirits and wine.

Saunders was very careful not to denigrate Bell's as a company. In fact, he was quite effusive in his praise of the firm. The nearest he would get to criticism was to state that Bell's had lost its way. He argued that Bell's was indeed an efficiently run company, for which one had to thank Miquel: however, it was not effective in the marketplace, especially overseas, which was equally the responsibility of Miquel. And basic commonsense told one that effectiveness, not efficiency, is the key to corporate success. In his first week, in

Scotland, Ernest Saunders made a lot of friends. He gained the initiative and was never to lose it throughout the 10 week struggle that ensued. One of the major reasons for this was the more or less inept handling of the affair by Miquel.

If Guinness's initial assault on Bell's went off like clockwork, then Miquel's behaviour was an object lesson in how not to fight off a takeover bid. When he received news of the Guinness bid, in a Chicago hotel room, Miquel began making a series of errors from which he never recovered.

First, apparently in the belief that such a bid for his company was quite ridiculous, he refused to cancel appointments in New York and return to Scotland. Secondly, after flying back five days later, he gave a press conference, not in Scotland, but in London. Thirdly, the press conference was at 4 p.m.—a time journalists want to be writing not listening. Fourthly, the press conference was held in London's west end, instead of near Fleet Street, necessitating a half-hour journey each way for the journalists. Fifthly, he gave exactly the same story to the Scottish journalists the next day in Scotland and finally, in handling the press Miquel behaved in an overbearing and autocratic way.

It was in stark contrast to the well-mannered, articulate media briefings given by Saunders. In a charged atmosphere Miquel issued an uncompromising rebuttal of Saunders' claim that a Guinness takeover would be good for both Bell's and Scotland. Such a takeover would be a disaster he claimed, 'it would be a catastrophe for the proper marketing and development of Bell's products and could lead to redundancies. It would not be good for the Scottish whisky industry or Scotland in general. I personally would find it impossible to work under the Guinness regime as I have seen it operating in the licensed trade'.

Miquel also predicted that many senior managers would share his feelings and would leave Bell's rather than work for a Guinness subsidiary. Of those that remained, their morale would be low and the 12-hour days that were demanded of them would no longer be the norm. All this would result in falling sales and inevitable redundancies. He then went on to defend Bell's record, pointing to the company's 21 per cent share of the domestic whisky market and the potential inroads to be made in the US through the newly purchased Wellington distribution chain. There then followed a counter-attack on Guinness, with references to that company's own poor performance in the American imported beer market (where Guinness's market share had only risen from 1.6 per cent to 1.7 per cent between 1980 and 1984) and its share of the UK beer market which he claimed was stagnant at 6 per cent.

Neither press conference was a public relations success. Miquel, clearly uncomfortable and oversensitive, was thought by many to see the bid for Bell's as an attack on himself. His touchiness was amply demonstrated by his dressing-down a television crew in London who interrupted him whilst in full flow. The conference ended with Miquel saying that he had no intention of meeting Saunders as they had nothing to discuss, declaring: 'There is no price which is acceptable from Guinness for the control of Arthur Bell'.

On Friday 21st June Miquel returned to Scotland for a meeting with fellow Perth based company General Accident, Bell's biggest shareholders. He then went on to Edinburgh, where he and Saunders gave rival press conferences in hotels only a few hundred yards apart. Miquel's briefing was merely a re-hash of his London defence, consisting mainly of heavy doses of statistical abuse refuting the Guinness claims. He said that he felt no personal animosity against Saunders, but cast doubt on the claim that he was some sort of marketing genius; 'When he has 20 per cent of the beer market in the UK, I shall call him a marketing wizard'.

Miquel attributed Guinness' recent successes to nothing more than cost cutting exercises, claiming that its healthy balance sheet had more to do with rationalisation and redundancies than with market penetration, increased sales and brand building. He then launched into a wild personal attack on Saunders. Reminding his audience of his 30 years service with Bell's, he pointed out that Saunders 'had never been around long enough with any company to correct his mistakes'. He reiterated his belief that the two men had nothing in common and therefore any meeting between them would be pointless.

In bringing the debate around to personalities and not policies, Miquel was making a grave error. The reason why Saunders had not spent 30 years in one place was because too many heavyweight corporations wanted his talents; and those talents included the ability to deal with third-rate attacks on him as a manager.

Miquel should also have been aware that by bringing in the personal element he was creating a rod for his own back; he had never been the most popular man in Scotland and this sort of tactic would do little to alter that. It merely served to legitimise any personal attack Saunders might wish to make on Miquel. Not that Saunders did. He was too skilled a tactician to resort to such an attack so early in the day. Instead, he countered by pursuing a softer, more gentle line, concentrating on the issues and eschewing rhetoric. He replied, 'I would have thought this a serious matter and one ought to be adult about this'.

Saunders had neatly managed to hold himself up as a model of sweet reason compared with Miquel. He professed that he would like to discuss the takeover with Miquel, 'on a man to man basis, and in private, I'd like to explain to Mr Miquel why this merger is such a logical move'.

On Tuesday 25th June, Miquel gave his first clear demonstration of what one observer described as 'his remarkable propensity to shoot himself in the foot at every opportunity'. Having publicly declared on two separate occasions that he had no intention of meeting Saunders, Miquel was persuaded by Henry King, Miquel's personal lawyer and a non-executive director of Bell's to meet Saunders at Bell's own Piccadilly Hotel in London. After the meeting, both men declined to make any comment save for the usual cliché that 'discussions had been full and frank'. In actual fact, most of the meeting had been devoted to drafting a mutually agreed statement to be issued afterwards. It was never completed, and the only benefit which Saunders was able to gain was a first hand impression of just how hard Miquel would fight to retain what he saw as his company.

Whilst in London, Miquel took the opportunity to meet a group of Scottish MPs whose constituencies contained distilleries to brief them on Bell's position. He stated once again that were the Guinness bid to be successful, senior Bell's executives would lose their motivation, morale would fall and efficiency and productivity would suffer. Two Conservative MPs, Bill Walker, the Member for North Tayside, and Alex Pollock, Member for Moray and Nairn, took Miquel's prognostications very seriously. Walker appealed to Scottish institutional shareholders in Bell's to consider the offer very carefully. Whilst admitting that they might very well make a short-term killing by accepting the offer, he argued that they would be jeopardising their own future and 'undermining the very basis of their own existence by switching away from a uniquely Scottish company'. Pollock was even more taken with the Scottish rhetoric handed to him by Miquel. He commented, 'It was heartening that his prime concern was with the promotion of Scotch whisky, both at home and abroad, rather than with ancillary activities. On present information I hope all shareholders will think very carefully before putting at risk a well-established success story for Scotland'.

Saunders busied himself with preventing the bid being referred to the Monopolies Commission. He was at pains to point out to the press that Guinness owned neither a distillery nor any tied houses, so there would be no threat to the sales of Bell's whisky in existing outlets. He also promised that there would be no redundancies in Scotland. That evening was spent putting the final touches to the submissions due at the Office of Fair Trading on Thursday. The list of 'interested parties' was to contain a bombshell for Miquel.

On Friday 28 June, the formal offer document posted by Guinness to Bell's shareholders was made jointly by Morgan Grenfell and Noble Grossart. This endorsement by a pillar of the Scottish business community was a major blow to the Scottish institutional support in which Miquel placed so much faith, yet had done little to cultivate. A Noble Grossart director, Peter Stevenson, was quick to defend his bank's decision: 'The arguments for the Guinness bid very strongly outweigh the arguments against. Bell's facing problems at home and overseas and it doesn't seem to be finding a credible strategy to overcome them. Its whole management style is unchanged from the one that was successful in the 1970s.'

And in a sideways swipe at Miquel he added, 'Level headed people will respect the decision we have made'. The wooing of the Scots had begun in earnest.

The offer document itself contained few surprises. The initial Guinness bid of nine of its new ordinary shares for every 10 Bell's ordinary shares, with a 225p cash alternative, was now supplemented by an 80p cash offer for Bell's 400,000 cumulative preference shares. The rhetoric in the document was the by now familiar refrain that after a decade of growth Bell's had lost its sense of direction and motivation. There was also another attempt to allay fears that a Guinness takeover would lead to redundancies and a loss of management control. Guinness guaranteed that there would be no job losses within Bell's, and promised that the company would 'continue to be managed from Perth as an autonomous company subject only to overall strategic decisions'.

With what seemed to be becoming a very bad habit, Miquel was not in Perth to reject the offer. He was in London recruiting the merchant bankers S.G. Warburg to join with Henry Ansbacher to fight off the bid. A company spokesman firmly rejected the Guinness overture on his behalf. He gave short shrift to Saunders' assessment of Bell's current lack of direction. 'If Mr Saunders thinks we have lost our way, then he must have been looking at another company. It is arrant nonsense. Bell's is run on a very effective, efficient, lean basis. There's no fat here at all.'

The following week or so witnessed a lull in the action as Bell's set about producing its formal rejection of the Guinness offer. The only real flurry of activity concerned allegations levelled by Bell's against Morgan Grenfell its former merchant banker now working for Guinness. These allegations had been raised by Bell's in the first few days of the takeover bid, when they demanded that Morgan Grenfell, who had worked for them for nearly 20 years, should play no further part in the takeover. Miquel complained to the Takeover Panel about Morgan Grenfell's involvement with Guinness the day after the bid was announced. He met with little joy: the situation was unprecedented, but the Panel accepted Morgan Grenfell's claim that they had terminated their relationship with Bell's in February 1983 and as such there was no breach of conduct involved with them acting for Guinness.

Lord Spens, by this time head of corporate finance at Bell's merchant bank adviser Henry Ansbacher, but formerly of Morgan Grenfell, was appalled that Morgan Grenfell should act in a hostile manner to Bell's. Morgan Grenfell had advised and acted for Bell's for over 20 years and had handled their public flotation in 1971. Miquel certainly considered himself a Morgan Grenfell client, and as recently as December 1984 when he had been warned by Ian Watson of the *Sunday Telegraph* that Saunders was stalking his company, had consulted the bank about it. He had asked Christopher Reeves, the chief executive, if this were true. Reeves had denied it and had told him that Morgan Grenfell would not act hostilely towards him.

When the bid had been announced on Friday, 14th June, and Ansbacher had been appointed as advisers, they immediately sought an injunction to prevent Morgan Grenfell from acting for Guinness. This was not pursued.

Ansbacher then advised taking the case to the Takeover Panel. Lord Spens is fiercely critical of their ruling and the manner in which it was reached. Lord Spens was appalled 'You have got to remember that the Takeover Panel was set up by merchant bankers for the good of merchant bankers. When they heard that Bell's had only spent

£20,000 with Morgan Grenfell in the last two years and that Guinness had already spent £6 million that was the end of the case.'

Here the matter rested until the first week of July when the Tory MP Bill Walker, who had already set himself up as the champion of Bell's, raised the issue in the House of Commons. He claimed that he had evidence that refuted Morgan Grenfell's claims that their relationship with Bell's had ended in 1983, and that the bank had in fact been involved in the takeover of the Gleneagles Hotel Group, and had even been consulted since then. Mr Walker was scathing in his criticism of the Takeover Panel: 'I believe that Parliament and Ministers should now be given the opportunity to see the paper outlining Bell's case as it was presented to the panel.'

He continued, 'I am most disturbed and unhappy that a company such as Bell's, who are a model employer and whose sales have increased every year for the past 15 years should be at risk and who, it would seem, have not been given justice by a self-regulating City body'.

Walker's efforts were not applauded in some quarters. Peter Stevenson of Noble Grossart riposted, 'Mr Walker should sit down, stop talking, and look at the facts proposed in this merger. His attacks on Morgan Grenfell are totally inaccurate and, more importantly, are distracting people from the real and serious issue of whether the Guinness offer is good for Bell's and good for Scotland'. It was, in many ways, still an age of innocence.

The concern of Mr Walker excepted, Miquel was having little success in organising a coherent Scottish lobby which would be vocal in the defence of Bell's. Paradoxically it was Saunders who, in a quiet, understated way, was giving the issue the Scottish dimension which Miquel had mistakenly taken for granted. Saunders frequently commuted between London and Scotland to elaborate on his basic message that a Guinness takeover would benefit a large sector of the Scottish economy as a whole. He was also photographed in Scotland with his wife Carole and youngest son. The message seemed to be falling on increasingly receptive ears. If Saunders was not being heralded as a white knight, neither was he having doors slammed in his face. Some Scottish institutional shareholders had already disposed of a proportion of their Bell's holdings, and there was a flurry of activity on the stock market in the first week of July. On Friday 5th alone, over a million Bell's shares changed hands, largely as a result of speculators trying to gain a belated advantage from Guinness' initial bid. The battle was still only three weeks old, yet some financial writers were already prophesying that only a referral of the bid to the Monopolies Commission or the appearance of a rival bidder could prevent the ultimate capture of Bell's by Guinness.

On Friday July 12th Bell's shareholders received a well produced glossy brochure which constituted Bell's formal rejection of the Guinness bid. The document contained both jam today and the promise of jam tomorrow. The jam today came in the form of not one photograph of Raymond Miquel in the whole brochure, the first time such an omission had occurred in over 15 years. The jam tomorrow was a promise to shareholders of a 50 per cent dividend increase if they resisted the 'wholly inadequate and unacceptable' Guinness bid. Miquel predicted pre-tax profits in excess of 1984's £35.2 million, with a dividend forecast of some 7.2p per ordinary share.

The document then went on to defend Bell's record, both at home and overseas, and launched an attack on Guinness under Saunders. In an attempt to defend Bell's marketing skills, a favourite Saunders target, Miquel made reference to a singularly specious piece of data: in an independent whisky brand awareness survey conducted the previous month 44 per cent of those interviewed named Bell's. The significance of this was, of course, negligible: Saunders could rightfully claim that Guinness had an international brand recognition second only to Coca-Cola, and doubtless if, in 1940, a representative sample of Londoners had been asked to name a notable German many of them would have said Hitler. The fact was meaningless, yet Miquel, in a barely disguised reference to Wood Mackenzie, claimed that, 'These are facts, not the opinions of some broker'.

It was another example of the whole episode beginning to disappear behind a barrage of statistical claim and counter-claim. The attack on Guinness was no less strident. Miquel attacked the company's past performance, its marketing expertise and the competence of its management, claiming that Guinness was heavily dependent on outside consultants. (Saunders, somewhat disingenuously given the Bain connection, dismissed this last point as 'just a joke'.) The document went on to say: 'Guinness has been and still is suffering from a period of turmoil within its business and mistakenly believes that the acquisition of a company of the quality of Bell's will resolve its problems. Your board urges shareholders not to allow the quality of Bell's to be diluted by the problems of Guinness'.

Saunders seemed genuinely dumbfounded by some of the assertions made by Miquel and the overall tone of the rejection document. He commented, 'It surprises me that the Bell's document shows that the company doesn't seem to realise it has problems. We know brand awareness is high, but brand image is weakening. That's the underlying reason for the decline in its market share'.

Saunders went on to accuse Bell's of avoiding the key issues at stake, which in turn took Miquel by surprise. 'If these aren't the key issues' he retorted, 'what the hell is running a company all about?' Whatever the two men might say in print and in public, the final arbiter of their various truths was the stock market. It seemed unimpressed with the quality of the defence offered by Bell's in their rejection document: shares in the company remained stable, whilst shares in Guinness rose by 4p to 350p. For the first time, Guinness's 9 for 10 share offer matched exactly the 225p cash alternative. Increasingly, Miquel was pinning his hopes on the Guinness bid being referred to the Monopolies Comission. It was not to be.

On Tuesday 23rd July 1985, Miquel received a blow which lesser men might have considered mortal; Norman Tebbit, then the Secretary of State for Trade and Industry, finally announced that there would be no Monopolies Commission investigation into the Guinness bid. The decision came as no great surprise to anyone, save perhaps Miquel who was bitter in his denunciation of the government: 'The government could have been more supportive, but they have shown that they are not interested in successful companies which increase their exports, raise their profits and employ people. They have not taken account of employment factors or regional factors here. But we can fight this bid off on our own.'

Most others, including the stock market, did not share Miguel's confidence. Some speculators reasoned that Guinness would now move in to administer the *coup de grâce* with a raised bid. Accordingly, Bell's shares gained 10p to stand at 246p, easily out-reaching the 225p value of the 9 for 10 share offer. As the day's trading drew to a close, there was an atmosphere of brinkmanship on the floor of the stock exchange, with some brokers expecting Guinness to announce a one-for-one share bid. However, Saunders was in no rush to play his hand, as he had made clear earlier that day, 'Bell's has obviously lost its way, and has no credible arguments that could possibly justify an increased offer'.

However, he did not declare the Guinness bid as a final offer, which would have left him with no room for manoeuvre. Instead, a third closing date for the bid was set for 6th August. With just over a week to go before the expiry of the third deadline, Guinness brought its heavy artillery in to bear on Bell's shareholders. This was a document which they called a summary of the key issues involved in the takeover, reiterating the, by now familiar, Guinness arguments under headings like 'Bell's has lost its way', 'Bell's credibility?' and—in case anyone was in any doubt as to who has issued the document—'Why Bell's needs Guinness'. However, inside the velvet glove of corporate regeneration lay the iron fist of an appeal to the naked self-interest of shareholders.

Bell's shareholders had been assiduously wooed by both sides, but their constant nightmare was that Guinness might tire of the game and look for easier pickings elsewhere. Should this happen, then the shareholders would be left with nothing but happy memories and a return to the pre-bid market price. If any of them were unaware of this, then the Guinness document spelt it out for them: the Bell's share price, it stated, 'has substantially underperformed the *Financial Times* Actuaries All Shares Index between its peak on 17th February 1983, and 14th May 1985. Nothing that Bell's has said or written since our offers were announced appears to have altered the stock market's fundamental perception of Bell's. What, therefore, do you think will happen to the value of your investment if the Guinness offer is withdrawn through lack of acceptances by Bell's shareholders?'.

Whilst Bell's shareholders were left to digest that little nugget, the mud-slinging between Miquel and Saunders continued apace. This time it centred around yet another set of statistics and counter-statistics. Guinness claimed that brewing industry figures showed a 5 per cent rise in the sales of Guinness beers in the first half of 1985. With a tedious inevitability, Miquel riposted by waving another sheaf of statistics—emanating from the Brewers Society—that showed a decline in the Guinness market share from 5.4 per cent 4.2 per cent between 1979 and March 1985. Saunders was quick to respond, 'This is childish' he asserted. 'Sales of draught Guinness have achieved their highest volume growth for over 15 years. It is a remarkable case history of brand turnaround. Mr Miquel should have concentrated on a credible plan to turn around his own declining brand.'

Bell's bounced back. A City adviser to Miquel retorted, 'it should be a matter of concern to Guinness shareholders that Mr Saunders should regard independent research statistics of this importance as

1.   Lord Iveagh, the foremost representative of the Guinness family on the company board. He was to say of Saunders, 'Once a friend, always a friend. But I do feel let down.'

2.   Jonathan Guinness, another family representative on the board. He was alleged to have said, 'Saunders must step down.'

3.   Raymond Miquel, the chief executive of Bell's. He said, 'We are amateurs at this game.'

4.   Ernest Saunders, chief executive and then also chairman of Guinness. He convinced many people of his skill and vision.

5. Carole Saunders, wife of Ernest Saunders. Not sure whether she was househunting in Edinburgh, Oxfordshire or near Heathrow.

6. Charles Fraser, the Edinburgh lawyer. He became a director of Bell's after the takeover and was to be a non-executive director at Guinness. Almost above all others he was to be sadly disillusioned by Saunder's behaviour.

7. Peter Tyrie, director of Bell's, responsible for Gleneagles Hotel. He did not see eye to eye with Miquel and defected to Saunders.

8. Angus Grossart, chairman of merchant bank, Noble Grossart. He worked with Saunders in 1985, against him in early 1986 and tried to salvage some pieces in mid 1986.

9.  James Gulliver, chairman of the Argyll Group. He had plotted carefully the capture of Distillers. He made one very expensive mistake but might still have won in a fair fight. Some say he's better off with Safeway than Distillers.

childish'. What was really a matter of concern, of course, was the sheer irrelevance of the whole exchange. What was important to Bell's shareholders was the 225p offer price for their shares—not how much or how little Guinness stout had been drunk over the past six years.

Miquel's next move was more reasonable. On 5th August he announced that Bell's profits for the year ended June 1985 would be even bigger than the forecast given in July, being 'somewhere in the order of £37.5 million, with a dividend of not less than 9.2p a share'. The announcement was nicely timed, coming on the very day that Bell's were legally bound to hand in their formal rejection to the Takeover Panel, the stock exchange and Morgan Grenfell. The forecast gave Miquel a platform from which to denounce the Guinness bid. With a £21.5 million after-tax profit the £297.6 million Guinness offer valued Bell's at a mere 13.8 years earnings. Bell's shares climbed 5p to 241p on the strength of the report and speculation that Guinness would increase its bid. Saunders made what capital he could out of Miquel's last minute timing by putting it down to the consequences of an impending boardroom split. But it was becoming obvious to him that the time had come to administer the *coup de grâce*.

## The Final Push

The day after Miquel was brandishing Bell's 1984/85 profit forecasts Ernest Saunders made his final move. He raised his bid from £297.6 million to £370 million: the new terms were four Guinness shares for every five Bell's shares, with a cash price of 245p in respect of each Bell's share. Although Guinness' initial offer had been fairly generous, for some weeks past the stock market had been hinting that the terms needed a slight 'beefing up' to secure the prize. Guinness could take a hint. The new terms valued Bell's at a significantly higher level than it could ever hope to command without the presence of takeover hype. Few whisky industry observers considered Bell's shares to be worth anything more than 200p on fundamentals, and the financial press were coming out openly on Guinness' side.

An equally valuable ally to the Guinness cause came in the form of Peter Tyrie, the Bell's director, who publicly broke with Miquel over the latter's rejection of the new Guinness offer. There had never been much love lost between Miquel and Tyrie since their days as adversaries during Bell's takeover of the Gleneagles Group. (Relations had deteriorated further when Miquel tried constantly to interfere in the running of the Gleneagles Hotel. On one occasion he said to Tyrie, 'Look I know more about running hotels than you do. I have been in more of them') However, one of Bell's few strengths in its defence against Guinness was the solid front presented by its board. This had now been broken. Tyrie was angry that Miquel had rejected the new offer without consulting the rest of the board. Accordingly, on Wednesday 7th August 1985 he said publicly that he would advocate Bell's shareholders accept Guinness' terms. Miquel was incensed, and two days later convened a board meeting to demand an explanation from the rebel director.

The *Sunday Times* on Sunday 11th January 1987 carried a large article by its Insight team on the front of the Business News section of the newspaper which made a great deal of the Tyrie defection. They showed that Tyrie had had meetings with Noble Grossart, Guinness's advisers, with Quayle Monro, financial advisers in Edinburgh and even with Ernest Saunders. They said that Bill Walker, the Conservative MP for North Tayside, (a man who implacably opposed the Guinness bid for Bell's) was arguing that Tyrie's meetings with Guinness and Noble Grossart were 'improper and amounted to an act of "skulduggery"'. They made much of Tyrie's costs—circulating the Bell's shareholders—of £50,979.61 and the fact that these were eventually paid by Guinness. They also mentioned that Morgan Grenfell supplied printed labels of all the Bell's shareholders.

The Tyrie defection was certainly another nail in the coffin of Bell's independence but, in spite of allegations to the contrary, it would seem to have been no more than an unhappy director making his views known.

Whatever explanation Tyrie might have given at the time is not known; what is clear is that Miquel finally realised the hopelessness of his situation. After a five hour board meeting on Friday 9th August 1985, from which Tyrie was excluded, the board issued a brief statement giving up the fight to stay independent but publicly seeking a white knight. The statement read that the Bell's board were: '. . . unanimous in concluding that in their view the revised final offer by Guinness does not reflect a full valuation for Bell's. They believe that it is their duty to secure the highest possible price for the company which is compatible with the protection of the Bell's business and employees, and consequently Bell's are seeking an alternative offer'.

Bell's had no definite prospect in mind, but it was apparent that for some weeks they had been scouring the world for a likely candidate.

This revelation did their cause no good. Where, Guinness asked, was their much vaunted 'Scottishness' now?

With Bell's apparently down, Ernest Saunders flew north on August 11th to put the boot in. He arrived in Glasgow and warned Bell's shareholders that as Miquel had put the company up for auction they should stop gambling with its future and accept the Guinness offer. The appearance of Saunders seemed to breathe new life into Miquel: he claimed that the statement made by the Bell's board on the previous Friday had been grossly misinterpreted, and that the board, always excepting Tyrie, were unanimous in their belief that the company should remain independent. Asked if this meant that Bell's no longer sought an alternative bidder, Miquel did little to clear up the confusion. 'I'm not saying that either,' he replied. 'It is important for the shareholders to get what they want.'

Saunders was clearly exasperated by this development. He managed to retain his singularity of purpose, however: 'I really don't think this confusion in the Bell's board about what they did or didn't mean on Friday should lull the individual shareholder into taking a gamble not to accept the firm offer Guinness has placed on the table. If someone were to emerge and our bid lapsed, the shareholders would have lost £1 a share and our guarantee on employment would have disappeared'.

He went on to warn Bell's shareholders to be wary of a rival bid from assset strippers, pointing out that the Gleneagles Group represented a tempting target. When pressed about his own plans for the hotel group should Guinness be successful, he gave an unequivocal guarantee that apart from the Piccadilly Hotel in London the rest of the group would not be for sale by Guinness. We shall see later how much that promise meant.

The following days were characterised by rumour, speculation, and disarray in the Bell's camp, all of which was hugely enjoyed by Guinness. It was now merely a matter of time, and as far as they were concerned the frenzied activity at Bell's was merely the final twitching of a dying man. Miquel had been forced to retract his earlier statement concerning Bell's profit forecast; Peter Tyrie had publicised his intention of selling his own 40,000 shareholding in Bell's to Guinness; the Bell's board were voicing aloud their wishful thinking about a 'white knight' who would allow Bell's the right measure of independence', and Bill Walker MP had found another finance house, Quayle Munro of Edinburgh, which should be investigated by the

Takeover Panel. Guinness made hay while the sun shone, contrasting its own calm reason with every confused move in the Bell's camp.

There was, however, to be one last fright. On 18th August there seemed a strong likelihood that another bidder might emerge in the shape of Rothman's. Sources close to Miquel claimed that meetings had taken place at Rothman's instigation. Despite denials by Sir Robert Crichton-Brown, Rothman's executive chairman, and a taciturn 'No comment' from Miquel the threat was still sufficiently worrying to Guinness for Saunders to issue its toughest statement thus far. If the rumours were correct, it began, 'It is not more than a desperate last-ditch delaying ploy which would fail. Bell's shareholders will see straight through Mr Miquel's scheme, which has only one aim in view—to secure his precarious personal position and allow him free rein to continue on his outdated and disastrous course.'

Guinness may have suffered a mild attack of panic, but the speculation about a third party was something they had prepared for. In fact, Saunders had drawn up a list of names being bandied around the City, and he was ready with a counter-attack for each of them. That the name to emerge was Rothman's, with its strong South African links, simply meant that he did not have to worry too much—help was to come from other quarters.

Two days after the flurry of speculation concerning a possible counter-bid by Rothman's, David Steel MP, Leader of the Liberal Party, publicly came out in support of Guinness. Rothman's South African links obviously troubled Mr Steel, who had long been an opponent of apartheid. Mr Steel condemned any proposed involvement between Bell's and Rothman's as 'the height of cynicism'. Despite the fact that a bid by Rothman's was by now verging on the realms of fantasy, Mr Steel strongly urged Bell's shareholders to accept the Guinness offer. It was a public relations coup of the highest order for Saunders.

The closing date for the Guinness bid had been set for Friday 23rd August. Nothing short of a miracle could save Bell's, and the company had to admit that no such miracle was on the horizon. Exasperated by the speculation over a rival bidder, Tony Richmond-Watson of Morgan Grenfell had written to Bell's pointing out that under rule 19.4 of the City Code on Takeovers any information provided by Bell's to a rival bidder must also be given to Guinness. The Bell's board replied that no such information had been given, an admission that there was no other interested party. It was a clever move by Morgan

Grenfell—they were fast acquiring a reputation for clever moves in takeover battles.

The final decision on the future of Bell's lay in the hands of around 80 institutional and some 6,000 individual shareholders. Bell's maintained that they were confident that they would win the day, but by now it was obvious that they were whistling in the dark. City opinion gave them not the slightest chance. If anything more were needed to convince those who still wavered, it came from Alan Gray, an analyst and whisky industry expert with the Glasgow brokers Campbell Neill. Gray, although 'reluctant to see the disappearance of yet another independent Scottish company', recommended the acceptance by Bell's shareholders of the Guinness cash and shares offer. Like so many other analysts, Gray had finally allowed the realities of the situation to overcome what sentimental barriers he may have at first erected. Should the Guinness bid be rejected, he pointed out, then Bell's shares would fall as low as 180p.

By 3 p.m. on Friday 23rd August, the deadline set for acceptance of the Guinness offer, it was obvious that Guinness had won a landslide victory. The acceptances processed by 3 p.m. totalled some 86 million ordinary shares or about 65 per cent of Bell's equity. When all the acceptances had been processed on the following Tuesday it amounted to 93.7 million of Bell's 132 million ordinary shares, some 71 per cent.

One of the last acts in the drama had been the acceptance by the Perth based General Accident which held around 12 per cent of Bell's shares. Their acceptance had been filed at 2.55 pm, and their 'defection' as Miquel saw it, left him feeling 'a bit depressed at being sold out by my friends'. It was left to the still energetic Bill Walker MP to deliver the most scathing indictment of General Accident: 'These people, who have made millions out of Bell's very fine performance down the years, have now sold Bell's down the river. The people of Perth won't forget what's happened'. General Accident declined to comment on its investment decision.

That night, the Guinness camp held a celebratory dinner in their newly acquired Piccadilly Hotel. Their table had been booked the previous day under an assumed name.

The fate of Raymond Miquel still hung in the balance. With the battle lost, Bell's had issued a dignified statement noting that Guinness had acquired a controlling interest in the company and hoping that they would continue to enhance the success Bell's had enjoyed in the past. But Miquel was keeping his silence. For his part, Ernest Saunders was being magnanimous in victory: he repeated the assertions he had made time and time again throughout the saga on the future of Bell's: 'Our objective is to build the Bell's business. The business will be managed from Perth and the management and workforce will be working with us to grow the business'.

Such a statement did not preclude Miquel playing some role in Bell's new organisation. Many, of course, were sceptical about Miquel's willingness to work under Saunders: he had publicly stated that he would find such a relationship difficult and the bitterness of the takeover had engendered a good deal of animosity between the two men. It was with some surprise, then, that after three days of meetings between the two men it was announced on 30th August that Miquel was to stay on as full-time chairman and chief executive of Bell's. Saunders had kept to the letter his promise that there would be no redundancies resulting from the takeover—so far.

# FOUR

## 'Distillers is a National Disgrace'

### The Promises Start to be Broken

However it may have appeared to the media, the Guinness acquisition of Bell's had run like clockwork and served as a textbook example of how a hostile takeover bid should be conducted. Saunders had masterminded a smooth operation, in which he had revealed all those facets of his personality which made him such a formidable opponent. By turn he was charming, forceful, attentive, authoritative and, most of all, he displayed a superb ability to identify and act upon opportunities as and when they arose. And in Raymond Miquel he had found an adversary who gave him an almost endless supply of opportunities.

What had Guinness gained? At the very least they had acquired, at slightly less than the true value, a distilling company which had been efficiently run by its chief executive and which had enormous potential for the future. It also had some very obvious problems. Those problems would be dealt with in typical Saunders style—through the introduction of marketing orientated managers into key positions (Miquel lasted less than three months at Bell's after the Guinness takeover), the identification of strategic business units and their subsequent development, and the ruthless divestment of anything that did not accord with Saunders strategic imperatives. What he might have said in the past, in the heat of a takeover battle when friends had to be made and kept, did not concern him once that battle was over. This was exemplified by the fate of the Gleneagles Hotels Group, which had cost Bell's £44 million. Saunders had stated that with the possible exception of the Piccadilly Hotel the group was not for sale. Between April 1986 and October 1986, Guinness sold the Piccadilly, Caledonian and North British hotels for a total of around £54 million. Takeover rhetoric, like election promises, went by the wayside in the face of a £10 million profit and the chance to retain the prestigious Gleneagles hotel.

As early as July 1985 at the height of Guinness's takeover battle for Bell's, Alick Rankin, the urbane chief executive of Scottish and Newcastle, had approached Saunders, whom he knew well, and suggested that he might want to divest himself of the hotels if his bid was successful. Saunders had agreed that this was possible, in spite of what he was saying publicly, and also agreed to give Scottish and Newcastle first refusal.

Rankin followed up this conversation after the successful takeover and Saunders confirmed that the whole situation was minuted. They would of course have to match any competitive offer. Rankin understood that and was happy with it. What he was not happy with was the fact that when negotiations did start for the sale of the North British and Caledonian hotels information about his bids seemed to leak out. Nor was he any more happy to learn that every time he bid he was beaten by Norfolk Capital whose chairman, Richmond-Watson, just happened to be a director of Guinness's merchant bank, Morgan Grenfell. It even got to the stage where Rankin telephoned Saunders to complain about the Dutch auction. Saunders listened and said he would telephone back. He did within half an hour to say that Norfolk Capital had made a higher bid than the one Morgan Grenfell Laurie had just told Rankin was the highest.

Rankin refused to make a higher bid and retired from the auction perplexed that Guinness could behave in such a way for the sake of half a million pounds or so, particularly when Scottish and Newcastle were one of Guinness' largest trading partners.

In securing Bell's, Guinness had gained something infinitely more valuable than a chance to revitalise the Bell's brands and make a quick 'buck' in the property market. By climbing inside 'the tartan ring' the company had put its foot on the ladder that would ultimately lead to a position amongst the real giants of the industry, those foreign combines whom Saunders had predicted would carve up the liquor world for themselves. When Jimmy Gulliver, chairman of the Argyll group, made his move for Distillers, some financial journalists suggested that given the vulnerability of the company, Saunders had set his sights too low and had acted too hastily in going for Bell's. Such commentators missed the point entirely: without the extra dimension Bell's gave Guinness, any designs Saunders may have had on Distillers would have been laughably unrealistic. The most important thing Guinness acquired in the takeover of Bell's was credibility.

## Distillers: An Enigma Comes under Scrutiny

Distillers is at once 'one of our best known and most mysterious of companies', wrote the *Observer's* Peter Wainwright when rumours about a takeover grew to more than a gentle hum. If anything, Wainwright was understating the case. In an age when communication was the buzz word on every chief executive's lips, the Distillers Co. Ltd maintained a silence that would have aroused the admiration of a Whitehall mandarin. Distillers was not in the communication game and took no steps to present a corporate image to the world at large. Given their immediate history this might have been understandable: equally, by taking on board some of the weapons of modern corporate management the company might not have made such an attractive target for the predators who gathered in 1985.

Distillers meant many different things to many different people. Some thought of it as being Scotland's largest company, a liquor empire built on impeccable worldwide brands like Johnny Walker whisky and Gordon's gin. To many others, the majority perhaps, Distillers was merely the company that played a large, and largely discreditable, role in the thalidomide drug tragedy.

57

The decision to diversify in the 1950s was part of a strategic plan quite common to companies which had identified the essential vulnerability of their narrow production base. Guinness, for example, attempted it, often with laughable results. In the late 1950s Distillers decided to enter the expanding pharmaceutical market. The result was, as Harold Evans, then editor of *The Times*, put it in 1973 'the greatest drug tragedy of our time'.

Distillers acquired the British rights to market thalidomide, generally known here as Distaval or Tensival, from its German originators Chemie Grueneuthal in 1957. The drug had been developed as a tranquiliser for women during pregnancy (one of its positive benefits was that it counteracted morning sickness) and it was prescribed as such by many doctors throughout Britain. Its most notable effect, however, was the large scale deformation it caused to the unborn foetus. From 1959 to 1961, when the drug was withdrawn, some 8,000 children were born with the deformities caused by the drug. The majority of them lacked either arms or legs: some lacked both and some died.

Their plight, and that of their parents, aroused the compassion of the nation. On the other hand it showed the complete inadequacy— and often incompetence—of both the legal system and the legal profession. And finally it earned for Distillers, through their own actions, the condemnation of many.

The first writ against Distillers alleging negligence over thalidomide and seeking damages was issued in November 1961. This opened the way for a further 61 writs to be issued during the next year: it also witnessed the complete inadequacy of certain parts of the English legal system and the uphill struggles endured by many to gain the most rudimentary form of justice. Due to 'various legal delays' the case did not reach trial until 1967. It was at this point, as is common in personal litigation, that Distillers made a settlement offer—if the litigants involved were to drop allegations of negligence then the company would pay the children 40 per cent of what they would have received *if* they had won their case in court. On the advice of their lawyers, the thalidomide victims accepted this out-of-court settlement. However, agreement soon broke down on the hypothetical 100 per cent damages from which the 40 per cent could be calculated. Two test cases were therefore taken to Court, and on the basis of the awards made to them a figure of around £1 million was paid to the children involved.

With the announcement of the award, over 300 new claims were entered. Distillers began to negotiate a settlement of these claims, and in 1971, when some of the victims were entering their teens, they put forward their proposal. A charitable trust was to be established which would receive £3.25 million over a 10 year period, about the equivalent of £8,000 cash compensation to each victim. Given that it was a charity, of course, no child would have an enforceable claim in law. Finally, it was a condition that all the parents must agree to the arrangement or it would be void.

In fact, six parents did not agree to the proposal, arguing that their children had a right to compensation and should not have to be means-tested to establish their eligibility for charity. These six individuals were taken to court by the solicitors of the majority of parents, and removed as 'the next friend' of their children, (which is to say they could no longer make legal decisions for them, this role now being taken by the Official Solicitor). This decision was subsequently reversed in the Court of Appeal, one of the few occasions during the whole affair when the forces of law appeared to be on the side of the victim.

Distillers then made a second, modified offer. They maintained the mechanism of the 10 year, £3.25 million trust, but also offered as an alternative a cash division for parental unanimity, substituting 'a substantial majority' instead. It was all becoming too much for the *Sunday Times*. In a three page article and a leader article on 24th September 1972, it commented: '. . . the thalidomide children shame Distillers. It is appreciated that Distillers have always denied negligence and that if the case were pursued, the children might end up with nothing. It is appreciated that Distillers' lawyers have a professional duty to secure the best terms for their clients. But at the end of the day what is to be paid in settlement is the decision of Distillers, and they should offer much, much more to every one of the thalidomide victims. It may be argued that Distillers have a duty to their shareholders and that, having taken account of skilled legal advice, the terms are just. . . . The figure in the proposed settlement is to be £3.25 million spread over 10 years. This does not shine as a beacon against pre-tax profits last year of £64.8 million and company assets of £421 million. This £3.25 million is not a large sum in the context of Distillers' commercial operations—a little less than 10 per cent of last year's after-tax profits, a little more than 1 per cent of the money made in the 10 years since thalidomide. . . .'.

The controlled invective of the *Sunday Times* cut through to the very heart of the issue. Whatever the legal niceties of the situation, many people felt that the company had a moral obligation to the victims of thalidomide. Not only did they seem to be shirking such a responsibility, they were also hiding behind the full, tawdry majesty of the English legal system in their attempts to prevent the *Sunday Times* from publishing details of the episode. It was, at the very least, an incredibly short-term and short-sighted view that the company had taken. Whether they were legally liable or not, the Distillers board should have had sufficient perception to realise that such an emotive issue would do irreparable harm to their corporate image. A generous settlement that did not have to be wrung out of them over a 10 year period might have gone some way to allaying public resentment towards Distillers.

If Distillers were incapable of seeing the damage to their image in the public eye, they might have been expected to notice the effect the episode was having on company morale. It has been suggested that the thalidomide tragedy and resulting scandal affected company morale so severely that it was a major factor contributing to Distillers' decline in the 1970s and 1980s. As one ex-manager reminisced: 'At times things got bad, very bad, and we'd all feel pretty down, a little bit ashamed and embarrassed by it all. The journalists on the *Sunday Times* weren't doing anything to make our lives easier, either. Not that they were ever anything but polite, but some of them could teach the "gutter-press" hacks a thing or two about leg-in-the-door interviews. So morale could really plummet on occasions. You've got to remember that this was the 1960s and the 1970s, when everyone suddenly discovered they had a social conscience. At drinks parties, that sort of thing, there was always someone whose ears would prick up if you mentioned exactly who you worked for and they'd launch into the standard diatribe. And you mustn't forget the poor kids—just because we worked for Distillers it didn't mean we were immune to the suffering—if anything we were more sensitive to it all. I know one or two young men, bright guys with good futures ahead of them, who packed the company in as a direct result of the thalidomide affair. You couldn't blame them'.

Whether or not the thalidomide episode and its effects on company morale was a contributory factor in the decline of Distillers, there can be no doubting the extent of the decline. In 1985, the company still had a very impressive two-fifths of the world whisky market, and whisky production accounted for just over 80 per cent of the group's business. But these impressive figures mark a very significant erosion from the position enjoyed by the company right up until the mid 1970s. In the 10 years to 1984, Distillers saw its share of the UK whisky market slump from 54 per cent to 15 per cent, with the virtual disappearance of a one-time brand leader such as Haig which went from 1.5 million cases sold in 1973 to 300,000 in 1984. In 25 years Distillers share of the whisky market had collapsed from 75 per cent to 15 per cent. More significantly, perhaps, was Distillers reluctance—or inability—to launch new lines. Added to this was the decision by the company in 1979 to withdraw Johnnie Walker Red Label from the UK market after a pricing dispute with the European Commission, leaving the field clear for Bell's and Famous Grouse.

Legal wrangles of one sort or another and the ossification of management structures and attitudes served to exacerbate the increasingly hostile trading environment Distillers faced. Like Bell's, the company found itself in an increasingly complex and fragmented world market which was experiencing an overall decline. Distillers found itself suffering intense competition in overseas markets it had traditionally seen as almost being home grown. In 1977 the world market for Scotch whisky had been 68 million cases. By 1984 it was 65 million, a decline of 3 million cases. Over the same period Distillers' share declined from 31 million cases to 23 million.

An example of increased competition was in Japan, a nation which had a peculiarly well developed taste for Scotch whisky, and where Distillers had enjoyed some notable successes. One such success, that of the company's White Horse brand, owed more to luck than judgment. The brand was immensely popular in Japan for reasons Distillers could never quite work out. It transpired that a white horse is a lucky symbol in that country. However, Distillers' market there was being increasingly penetrated by Japan's own Suntory brand and Hiram-Walker's Ballantines', an aggressively marketed product which was one of the first whiskies to be supported by aspirational lifestyle advertisements aimed at the younger market. Most ominously, in the summer of 1985, there emerged Sochu, a cereal based spirit which sold at 800 yen a bottle against the 4,000 yen for a bottle of whisky. This wreaked havoc in a lucrative market where Distillers was already fighting hard to maintain sales. Some people were of the opinion that the company's performance was the main reason behind the malaise of the Scotch whisky industry as a whole in the early part of the 1980s. Market analyst Tim Clarke, of Panmure Gordon certainly had few doubts: 'The extent to which the decline of the industry was the decline of the Distillers company is a very important point to make. It's an open question whether the industry could have been marketed better'.

## The Target

To its credit, Distillers prepared to enter the second half of the 1980s with some attempt at reorganising its marketing strategy, largely on the initiative of its chairman John Connell. There were aggressive moves in the Japanese market with the introduction of two brands targetted specifically at the Japanese. In the United Kingdom, Johnny Walker Red Label was relaunched and met with some modest success. The company also looked very carefully at the image of its products and examined ways of attracting younger consumers to Scotch whisky. One very interesting early experiment was the introduction of 'Johnnie Colada', a whisky-based cocktail which the company claimed was as popular as the more traditional piña colada favoured by younger drinkers.

But was it all a case of too little too late? The company continued to perform badly: pre-tax profits in 1984/5 were £236.2 million compared with a 1983/4 figure of £191.6 million and a 1982/3 figure of £200 million. And even such a relatively poor performance in 1984/5 was somewhat flattering: the company benefited from an expensive dollar. The prospects for 1985/6 were not so rosy. By August 1985 it was beginning to look even less rosy.

On the last day of August 1985, Michael Tare, writing in the *Financial Times*, summed up the Distillers predicament. 'One hundred and twenty-seven brands of whisky are produced by the Distillers Company Limited—but you cannot buy one of them in the pub across the road from this office. Drinkers no longer ask for Distillers' whiskies, in England at least, and Bell's and Famous Grouse sit alongside brewery house labels on the optics . . . the slump in UK market share to below 20 per cent illustrates just one of the problems that faces Mr John Connell, head of the empire that remains responsible for close on 4 in every 10 bottles of whisky produced. And it helps explain why so many people are prepared to believe that Distillers is a sitting duck for a predator'.

There were other less than subtle indications for those who paid more attention to market prices than market share. On 21st July,

Distillers shares stood at 285p; by the beginning of September they had risen sharply to 359p. There were the usual crop of rumours, and some of the names of the fancied bidders were mentioned. Prominent amongst them was Hanson Trust. However, they were at that time involved in a contested bid in the USA, and nobody seriously expected them to get involved in a war on two fronts. GEC, with a 3 per cent holding in Distillers, seemed a more likely candidate, and it later transpired that they had indeed been working with Argyll with a view to making a bid. GEC were to provide the money—they had their famous, almost notorious, cash mountain of £1.5 billion—and Argyll were to provide the management. GEC were being advised by Lazards, Argyll by Samuel Montagu. Sir Ian Macgregor, a director of Lazards and friend and neighbour of Jimmy Gulliver, had been encouraging Gulliver to make a bid and had promised help with Lord Weinstock, managing director of GEC.

As the rumours mounted, Argyll were ready to go but at the last minute GEC backed out. In his later frustration Jimmy Gulliver was to say, 'They had lost their bottle'. In fact in the last days of August 1985 there was gloom and despondency in the Argyll camp. They had been stalking their prey for a long time and had carried out the most detailed research (it is said that Gulliver knew more about Distillers than Distillers themselves). Now their financial backers had let them down. They felt that all their work had been for nothing. It led Jimmy Gulliver to utter the most expensive sentence in history, 'We do not intend to make an offer for Distillers at the present time'. But while Argyll were saying that and believing it to be true, their advisers, Samuel Montagu, were saying it could be done, that they could raise the money without GEC.

But the fateful remark had been made and for once the Takeover Panel acted firmly, imposing a three month ban on a bid, and stuck to its firmness, resisting all approaches from Argyll and its advisers to set this decision aside.

It is idle but not uninteresting to speculate on the cost of that sentence. At the time the Distillers' share price was around 350p and the company was valued at about £1.2 billion. A bid then of 450p or about £1.6 billion would probably have won the day. As it was, Argyll was forced to open with an offer of 513p, worth £1.8 billion, and of course by then Guinness had prepared themselves and the prize eventually went for 672p or £2.36 billion.

## The Grocer from Campbelltown

In 1986, at the age of 56, James Gerald Gulliver could with some justification claim to be amongst the most successful businessmen Britain had ever produced.

Born in the shadows of a whisky distillery in Campbelltown, Argyllshire, Gulliver was educated at the local grammar school and at Glasgow University, where he studied engineering. Between 1956 and 1959 he served in the Royal Navy on a short service commission, and began his effective management career as a consultant with Urwick Orr in 1961. It soon became apparent that Gulliver had the sort of talents that would take him to the very top: a sharp, incisive mind, an enormous appetite for work, drive, ambition, imagination and—most crucially—that curious and rare interaction of attributes that go to make up the entrepreneur. Above all things Gulliver was an entrepreneur and it was the entrepreneurial vision which he brought to the companies for which he worked.

In a speech he gave in September 1986, Gulliver gave an outline of his career and his own personal business philosophy. 'I was given my big chance by the late Garfield Weston (the chairman of Fine-Fare Supermarkets). He believed in total delegation to the chief executives of his various companies. If you faltered or failed you were fired, and I was the fifth chief executive of Fine-Fare in seven years. To take on this job was my first major career risk and I knew there was less than an even chance of survival. In the end I stayed for eight years and it was a stimulating time for me and I learnt a lot.'

It was also stimulating for some of the Fine-Fare directors. There are stories of some of them in tears as Gulliver lambasted them for their failings. But it was in the 1970s that Gulliver really proved his flair, guts and entrepreneurial spirit. Nowhere is this better illustrated than in his repurchase of the Oriel Foods company which he had started in 1973 and which he had sold to the American RCA Corporation. In Gulliver's own words, 'RCA were looking for £30 million for Oriel, Argyll was item capitalised at around £20 million, and their preferred purchaser was an industrial giant like ITT. RCA wanted a fast, unconditional cash deal. From my own sources, I knew there was a number of interested purchasers with offers on the table. Seizing the opportunity and without having time to consult our bankers, I flew to New York one Sunday, persuaded RCA, plus Lazards and Lehman Brothers to accept my private draft for

US\$250,000 as a non-returnable deposit against Argyll signing within 14 days an unconditional contract backed up by a bank guarantee. In view of the timescale and the risk, it was not practicable to ask the Argyll bankers before making the deposit. This certainly focussed my mind on the financing and also demonstrated to our bankers my own strong personal commitment to the deal.'

So Gulliver had the bottle even if GEC did not. He also had the personal financial commitment to his company with shares worth £17.4 million which the Distillers directors did not—the directors of Distillers had only 50,000 shares between them.

Those sound business and management practices had served Gulliver well throughout his career. In six years his application of them had built the Argyll Group up from scratch to an organisation which had sales of £1.76 billion, a stock market capitalisation of £670 million and a ranking as the sixty-fifth largest company in Britain. Argyll's pre-tax profits were £53 million and the number of employees 36,000. Gulliver's prey had a turnover of £1.27 billion, a market capitalisation of £1.85 billion and pre-tax profits of £236 million. It had 15,000 employees.

## Laying the Ground

James Gulliver delighted in referring to himself as a risk-taker, a man whose whole career had been built on the lucrative leap in the dark. It would, perhaps, be more accurate to say that he was a man willing to play the odds, especially when he could gain an edge over the opposition. The exact moment he decided that Distillers was decadent enough to fall into his hands and experience his unique brand of revitalisation is open to conjecture. The exact point when he actually started to work on it can be given with some accuracy—it all began in early January 1985 when Gulliver requested a list of those individuals whom insiders called the 'Scottish Mafia', a group of politicians, bankers and industrialists whose influence and favour could do much to reduce the 'knee-jerk Scottish factor' which emerged every time a Scottish company faced a takeover bid. Ironically, Gulliver had advised Saunders as to its importance, and Gulliver practised what he preached: in the early months of 1985, he set about giving himself an edge.

The 'Scottish Mafia', a term which, incidentally is not well liked by Scots in general, is split between Glasgow and Edinburgh, with the latter city enjoying the greater influence. Edinburgh still retains many important political functions, not least the office of the Secretary of State for Scotland, and its close-knit and canny bankers form a powerful group of their own. Lionel Barber, writing in the *Financial Times* characterised the situation thus: '. . . the interlocking friendships and directorships create a fierce *esprit de corps* which can be mobilised within the space of a few telephone calls when Scottish interests are threatened'*.

The strength of the lobby which could be aroused in Scotland was formidable. For example, in 1981, when the Royal Bank of Scotland faced two takeover bids, the lobby which finally forced the whole issue to the Monopolies Commission included the Scottish Office, the Bank of Scotland, the Scottish Development Agency, the Scottish TUC, Strathclyde University, *The Scotsman* and a horde of Edinburgh bankers, brokers and analysts. It was just such a powerful and well organised resistance that Gulliver needed to quash before it ever really gained momentum. Without it, he might just acquire Distillers; if he was confronted with it, he had no chance.

A superficial analysis of the situation might suggest that Gulliver would have aroused no such opposition. He was, after all, Scottish born and bred and fiercely proud of his origins—hence the name 'Argyll' for his greatest creation. He was a long standing member of the Scottish Council for Development and Industry, a governor of Scottish business in the community programme since 1983, and a visiting Professor at Glasgow University. He could genuinely claim far more in the way of Scottishness than the majority of the board of Distillers, most of whom preferred to spend their days in the home counties rather than north of the border.

Having said that, however, Gulliver was not exactly one of Caledonia's favourite sons. He had left Scotland at the age of 31 to devote his talents to making his substantial fortune in the greener pastures of England and Argyll was essentially an English company. He had also, on occasion, run foul of the Scotch whisky industry with the marketing of some of Argyll's brands, a few of which were notorious for their 'tackiness'.† It was necessary, then, for Gulliver to

---

*\*Financial Times*, 19th December 1985.

†*Private Eye* referred to Argyll's whiskies as 'Mickey Mouse' brands, and they do seem to have lacked a certain image. Argyll specialised in 'instant traditions' and names like Glen Scotia and Scotia Royal seemed to owe more to the creative copywriter than Scottish legend.

reacquaint himself with 'the great and the good' in Scotland, and this he did with a panache and alacrity remarkable even by his own standards. In March 1985, he became a member of the Scottish Economic Council which regularly met with George Younger, the Secretary of State for Scotland. Jimmy Gulliver had not merely gained the confidence of the Scottish mafia—he was well on his way to becoming one of them.

As the Argyll camp were gnashing their teeth with frustration during the autumn of 1985 what were the beleaguered directors of Distillers doing?

They were making some belated efforts to improve their own position. There was a flurry of activity as they stepped up their own search for a new acquisition and once again the rumours circulated that they would descend on the Scottish and Newcastle group. In fact, in November 1985 Alick Rankin, the chief executive of Scottish and Newcastle, had four meetings with the chairman of Distillers, John Connell, and agreement on a merger (in spite of what some of the press might have said no one of any calibre was going to allow themselves to be descended on by Distillers) was close. Rankin was prepared to accept that Distillers, very much the larger company, could take over Scottish and Newcastle but there would have to be rationalisation, i.e. job losses, and the board of Scottish and Newcastle would run the combined business. He told John Connell: 'Nine out of your 11-man board will have to go.'

That seemed to end the dialogue and towards the end of November Distillers appointed the prestigious Kleinwort Benson to man the ramparts against the forthcoming attack from the 'pesky' Gulliver. At the same time, Distillers brought forward the announcement of its interim figures, a slightly panicky move. This backfired on them completely, and was sufficiently counter-productive to earn them the lofty contempt of the financial world. Distillers declared that pre-tax profits had risen by 66 per cent to £124.3 million. Furthermore the timing of such an announcement, according to John Connell, the chief executive, had nothing to do with any impending bid by Argyll. The financial press did not even pay Mr Connell the courtesy of suggesting that the whole report might require a pinch of salt. The *Financial Times's* Lex column criticised the report, and it encountered considerable scepticism on the stock market. Many brokers considered that the figures had been inflated, pointing to the somewhat cursory analysis of divisional performance which made it impossible to pinpoint exactly from which sources such phenomenal growth had come. One city analyst summed up the general feeling with the remark 'All that glitters is not gold'. Distillers had certainly not done itself any favours with this ploy: by stretching the credulity of the stock market, they jeopardised the credibility of the full year profit forecast.

A more constructive move by the company was the appointment of Sir Nigel Broackes, the chairman of Trafalgar House, as a non-executive director. This reduced Distillers' vulnerability on a number of counts. The company knew that its ageing, absentee board would be one of the first targets for the abrasive, energetic Gulliver. At 51, Broackes was an injection of young blood into the boardroom; he was also an immensely capable and experienced take-over strategist, as well as being a highly skilled communicator. The company had already appointed the able and experienced American Bill Spengler as deputy chairman. They were ideal generals for the struggle that lay ahead—but was their late appointment enough to outweigh the years of lethargy that had gone before?

James Laurenson, chief executive of the Edinburgh bank, Adam and Co. was convinced by this move that Trafalgar House were going to be a white knight. He could remember that as long ago as 1971 when he had got to know Broackes quite well in his capacity as a fund manager at Ivory and Sime that Broackes had said to Victor Matthews in Laurenson's presence, 'We should take over Distillers'. Incidentally, Laurenson can also remember that at a lunch at Ivory and Sime in the early 1980s, shortly after the Paternoster restructuring at Woolworths, Charles Fraser, had said, 'What are we going to do about Distillers? We should do what they have done at Woolworths'.

## The Battle Commences

On Monday, 2nd December 1985, Argyll launched its bid for Distillers. It was ironic that the bid should be delivered to Distillers' head office in St. James's Square, London, while John Connell was sitting in the permanent Distillers suite in the Caledonian Hotel, Edinburgh. Angus Grossart was heard to grunt, 'Trust them to be in the right place for once at the wrong time'.

With Distillers' shares standing at 510p, the 523p-a-share bid valued the offer at £1.9 billion. The bid was not only remarkable for its size, but it also provided the City financiers with a taste of things to come with the advent of Big Bang, the scrapping of fixed commissions in the City of London which was then still more than a year away.

Gulliver's main problem had been the size of Argyll relative to its prey: in August, when Distillers shares stood at 290p, the gap between the two—although large—was not insurmountable. By December, Argyll's £670 million capitalisation was only one-third that of Distillers—a desperate situation which called for a highly innovative remedy. Argyll could not afford to put itself in a position whereby it would spend £40 or £50 million and then fail to capture the prize. Naturally, Gulliver had to turn to the banks and fortunately he found them far more flexible than they had been when he first started out on the entrepreneurial trail.

Argyll's principal financial advisers, Samuel Montagu and Charterhouse Japhet, had so arranged the £600 million loan finance and the £1.2 billion underwriting that those involved in the early stages of the bid would receive far higher than usual commitment and commission fees if the bid were to be successful. Were the bid to fail, or were it to be referred to the Monopolies Commission then they would receive virtually nothing. Argyll had calculated that if the bid failed or was referred they would be liable for less than £10 million in costs; were it to succeed, then total fees would be of the order of £74 million. It was what one might term 'contingency' financing, promising high rewards for success and nothing for failure—the safety net had been removed. Yet a number of institutions judged that the potential gains outweighed the obvious risks.

The finance for the Argyll bid consisted of three elements and was organised by Rupert Faure-Walker and his managing director, Ian Macintosh at Samuel Montagu. The first was £600 million of loan finance. Four banks took this risk, Samuel Montagu, Charterhouse Japhet, Midland Bank and Citibank. The banks agreed to provide an eight-year loan at a receiving rate of 0.35 per cent over the London Inter Bank Offered Rate (Libor) between years one to five. In years six to eight the rate would rise to 0.5 per cent. If the bid were to be referred to the Monopolies Commission or failed the banks would receive a much lower than normal commitment fee.

The second element was a slab of £500 million underwriting arranged by six institutions before the bid was launched and the third another £700 million of underwriting arranged when the bid was announced.

The same premium on success applied to the first £500 million of underwriting. If the bid succeeded, the fee would be 3 per cent, 1 per cent higher than usual. A new feature was that the underwriters would receive a package which would include a flat fee of just over 2½ per cent at the end of the bid period of up to 72 days instead of the normal fee up-front. If the bid failed or was referred they would receive a fee of ⅛ per cent or less.

Pulling in the necessary support for these terms proved less difficult than expected, but as one institution put it, 'In a takeover bid this size no one wants to be left out. These days it is a question of showing you can be a big player'.

Argyll's finance director, David Webster was delighted with the package. 'When Big Bang happens next year, these attitudes will become more pronounced with a premium being put on success'. It was a package putting a premium on success which was to be copied several times during 1986, most notably by Dixons in their bid for Woolworths.

One of the institutions involved was the Royal Bank of Scotland, Distillers' leading banker, which assumed part of the loan financing. Distillers was more than a little upset. Had the Royal Bank, where the company had banked for over a century, acted on a purely commercial basis, as chief executive, Charles Winter maintained, or were they acting as part of an alliance to oust Distillers of its often reviled management? It was a moot point, but Distillers did not spend overlong discussing it: the following week the company dismissed the Royal Bank, accusing it of great disloyalty, appointing the Bank of Scotland under Sir Thomas Risk as its new principal banker.

If Argyll's bid for Distillers was no great surprise, then Distillers response was even less so. The Distillers board rejected it out of hand, describing it as a 'sighting shot (which) is unwelcome and completely inadequate'. Bill Spengler was less courteous in his dismissal of Argyll's offer: 'Mr Gulliver deals in potatoes and cans of beans. He does not understand the whisky business'.

Nonetheless, the Argyll bid clearly had the company rattled, despite the time it had been given in which to prepare itself. The Argyll bid had been launched with every piece of professional advice the public relations industry could give it. Within a day of the bid being announced, the Office of Fair Trading, every relevant journalist, MP and institution and all Distillers' shareholders received a comprehensive brochure presenting Argyll's case and outlining the details of the offer—8 new shares and 10 new convertible shares plus £14.50 in cash for every 10 Distillers shares. This brochure combined a detailed attack on Distillers' abysmal performance in the previous decade with a glowing testimonial to Argyll's growth since its formation in 1979. Gulliver also sought to reinforce his case by announcing that the organisation created by the takeover of Distillers would have its corporate headquarters in Scotland, forming that country's largest private company and creating some 300 new jobs.

It took Distillers until the end of the month to prepare and produce their formal defence document. The days leading up to its issue were not passed in idle contemplation by either side, however. In the run up to Christmas 1985 neither side showed much inclination to leave the trenches and fraternise with the enemy in 'no man's land'. Instead, they both indulged in sniping attacks which looked set to make the biggest takeover bid in British history one of the nastiest as well. Gulliver was at pains to point out that the great Scottish institution which Distillers liked to think it was, was effectively run from England, where 13 of the 16-man-board (including Broackes) lived; he further added that only 20 per cent of the company's equity was held north of the border. He also drew attention to the proliferation of expensive properties the company held in central London (you could stand outside the RAC in Pall Mall and hit most of them with a wedge) including its headquarters in St James's Square and a separate office for the small Pimms operation in Pall Mall. No quarter was given to what was portrayed as the ineptitude of Distillers management in allowing the group to deteriorate so badly over the past 10 years; it was suggested that the board ran the company more like a gentleman's club than a business.

For their part, Distillers seemed content to pour scorn on the idea of an English based supermarket group taking over an aristocrat of the Scottish economy. There were also some rumblings concerning the overall economies of the deal; not merely the caddish behaviour—as Distillers saw it—of some financial institutions, but also whether it was feasible for Argyll to take Distillers over without incurring debts which would cripple the new grouping.

All these points were amplified in Distillers' official rejection document, issued by the company on New Year's eve. Distillers' defence centred around two main issues. On the one hand they branded Argyll as a drinks industry failure, saying, 'Argyll is unsuited for the stewardship of the Scotch whisky industry because the majority of its business is as a UK discount supermarket operator. Where Argyll is in the Scotch whisky industry it also trades predominantly on low prices.'

Furthermore, and not pulling any punches, the report added, that Argyll was, '. . . a buyer and seller of businesses . . . a discount retailer which compares unfavourably with its competitors.' More crucially, perhaps, the document claimed that the bid was debt-ridden: if it were successful it would lead to Argyll being geared at 100 per cent (compared with Distillers' 12 per cent) and as such, profits attributable to ordinary shareholders in the new group would fall by over 40 per cent.

Argyll responded quickly and predictably: another lavishly produced brochure attacked Distillers' past performance and ridiculed the company's claim that it was the leading light of the Scotch whisky industry. David Webster, Argyll's finance director, pointed out that Distillers had a tendency to ignore the beam in its own eye, commenting, 'In the first six months of 1985, Distillers reported a volume increase of only 10 per cent in the home market, while the increase in industry volume amounted to 16 per cent.'

Gulliver himself took the opportunity of a Glasgow press conference to accuse Distillers of hiding behind, '. . . highly selective and often meaningless statistics. Distillers now makes the astonishing claim that it is the most profitable spirits company in the world. Yet over the past six years Distillers' profits have failed to keep pace with inflation, earnings per share have fallen by 9 per cent and dividend growth has fallen behind inflation.'

Bill Spengler replied for Distillers, claiming that Argyll were not coming up with anything new: 'He (Gulliver) keeps knocking the past rather than looking at our present activity. We want to see what his plans are for the future.'

Distillers' own horizons, however, ran no further than whether or not the bid would be referred to the Monopolies Commission, as had been advocated by the Scottish Conservative and Unionist Industrial Committee. Such a referral was beginning to appear the company's best chance of salvation, as it would probably give them at least a six month period in which to improve their prospects. However, it was not to be, and in truth the company never had much of a case; a referral on the basis of balance sheet gearing was never watertight, and there were no other credible grounds—especially in the light of the government's much publicised commitment to open competition. It began to look as if Distillers would have to stand on its own two, rather flat, feet to withstand the onslaught of the 'ghastly grocer'.

On 9th January 1986, the Trade Secretary Leon Brittan advised by the Office of Fair Trading gave Argyll's bid the green light. Distillers were clearly losing. Gulliver, his finance director David Webster, the Glasgow ex-banker and Alistair Grant the ex-Unilever managing director of Argyll Foods had mercilessly exposed Distillers shortcomings. Even their code name for Distillers—Ascot—was picked because all the Distillers board seemed to live there. Kleinwort Benson now advised Distillers that a white knight was the only hope and engaged in a week of negotiations with Guinness and their advisers, Morgan Grenfell.

## Enter the White Knight

On 13th January, four days after Distiller's hopes for a referral to the Monopolies and Mergers Commission were dashed, Guinness issued its first profit figures since the takeover of Bell's. Allowing for the rhetoric commonly indulged in during a takeover, one could have forgiven Ernest Saunders if the Guinness figures were not quite of the magnitude predicted during the summer of 1985. In fact they were not—they were better. Group turnover for the year rose by 29 per cent to £1,188 million, an increase of £264 million. Interestingly enough, some £200 million of this increase came from the group's newly established retailing side. Profits rose from £70.4 million to a record £86 million, £3 million more than the predictions of the summer. Saunders's reign at Guinness was paying dividends that attracted the attention of more than just Guinness shareholders.

The Distillers board had been determined to fight on to maintain the company's independence right up until a crucial board meeting on 16th January. That meeting made it obvious to a majority of directors that a defensive merger was the only way they could fight off Argyll's bid. Informal contacts already existed between Distillers and Guinness—and between Distillers and a host of other companies for that matter—but on 13th January these informal contacts gelled into something more serious. The 16th January board meeting, which endorsed these contacts, was by all accounts not a pleasant affair. Although a majority of the board saw the logic of the Guinness connection, some of the older members could not be convinced. John Connell was himself unhappy about bringing in a third party. As Bill Spengler sympathetically put it, 'John felt the passing of independence more keenly than anyone. After all, his family had been involved in the Company for more than 60 years.'

Sir Nigel Broackes also felt that John Connell had expected to be chairman of the family business since he was at school, he was now chairman and he expected to stay as chairman. He also expected to pass the chair on to David Connell, his brother. But some of the directors could see that independence was gone. As one put it, 'That weekend was all about kicking John's arse.'

From 16th January onwards, there was a ceaseless flurry of activity between the two camps and the finance houses that would underwrite the record-making bid. Some of the work had already been done. According to Saunders, whatever doubts he may have harboured concerning the wisdom of the scheme disappeared during a visit to the opera, when a stream of bankers and fund managers urged him to proceed. By Friday, January 17th, most of the underwriting was in place, and all that remained was to give a final push to a still hesitant Distillers board.

## We Need a Chairman

It was on this day that Saunders telephoned Sir Thomas Risk who was at the London offices of the Bank of Scotland. Risk went over to Guinness' offices in Portman Square where he met Saunders and Roger Seelig, a corporate finance director of Morgan Grenfell and he was told of the plan to 'merge' Distillers and Guinness and was asked to be chairman of the new group. Risk turned down the offer, explaining that his job as Governor of the Bank of Scotland was a full-time one. Ernest Saunders however, produced his legendary charm and persuasiveness and Risk agreed to consult his colleagues.

As we shall see later, Risk, after consultation with his Bank of Scotland colleagues, eventually agreed to take the post. All that was needed now was the final push.

This push was administered in typical Saunders style. On the Saturday night prior to the official announcement of the bid, he drove to the home of John Connell overlooking Burhill golf course in Walton-on-Thames. Saunders drank Johnny Walker, whilst Connell drank Guinness. However, neither gentleman was there to indulge in mutual admiration of the two companies' respective brands: they were there to discuss their aspirations for the group which would arise from a Guinness-Distillers merger. Saunders also wanted to reassure himself that Connell was as committed to the merger as were the other Distillers directors. He was not in the mood for play-acting: he

informed Connell that if there was no firm agreement by Sunday night, the Guinness offer would be cancelled and the whole story would be broken to the press. As the two men sat drinking into the early hours of Sunday morning, the screw was turned even tighter. The early editions of the *Sunday Times* were already on the streets claiming that effectively the deal was as good as done (the deal had already been leaked to *The Times* and had appeared that morning). Whatever bargaining strengths Connell might have had were already fast disappearing. On his way home from Connell's house, Saunders rang Tom Ward to inform him that his *tête à tête* with Connell had resulted in everything for which he could have wished.

## The Maiden Says Yes

In the story the *Sunday Times* ran on the front of its Business News

75

entitled 'Guinness joins Scotch fray' it said, 'John Connell, the Distillers chairman, is prepared to stand down in favour of Ernest Saunders, chairman of Guinness.'

This was now becoming standard Saunders practice and as we shall see the technique was used again and again. Connell's position was effectively undermined. But of far greater significance was the demand by Guinness that Distillers bear the costs of the merger. This was to cause a great outcry and even legal action when it was revealed. At the Distillers board meeting the next day, Sunday, at which all the members were present, the board were initially split nine to five on whether to accept the 'merger' with Guinness and whether to accept the terms of paying Guinness' costs. Sir Nigel Broackes remembers that those opposed did seem to be the ones most likely to lose their positions (in the event of course, they all did).

After much discussion, the meeting broke up and many mini-meetings and telephone calls took place with Kleinwort Benson and every other adviser available. Eventually the board was reconvened in the evening at 9 p.m. and it was unanimously agreed that they must give a unanimous decision. The unanimous decision was—we agree to the terms, Sir Thomas Risk as chairman and Distillers will pay Guinness' costs.

Angus Grossart who had advised Saunders in the takeover of Bell's, but was now advising his old friend, Jimmy Gulliver, was appalled when he learnt of this indemnity on costs. (Guinness and Distillers did not of course publicly announce the indemnity but it was leaked, presumably by a disaffected Distillers director—some were obviously learning the effectiveness of carefully placed leaks.) He says that it was at that moment that he realised that this meant Saunders played to win, never mind the rules. Grossart was to be even more appalled when their appeal to the Takeover Panel allowed the ruse. In retrospect he thinks that it was then that Saunders thought he could get away with anything, particularly as far as the Takeover Panel were concerned. As we shall see he was right.

The full details of the bid were unveiled on Monday 20th January, and Saunders announced that, 'The two companies are a perfect fit, with Distillers' portfolio of quality brands and Guinness's reputation for drinks management'.

The terms of the Guinness bid were to be eight Guinness shares plus £7 in cash for every five Distillers shares, with a straight cash alternative of 585p per share: this was nearly £1 more than the Argyll cash alternative. The new company would be capitalised at around £3 billion, making it the tenth largest company in the country. The major stumbling block, of course, was the prospect of a referral to the Office of Fair Trading, a likelihood which had been stated quite blatantly in the financial press and which served to depress trading in Distillers shares which fell 5p to 562p.

A Guinness/Distillers combine would control approximately 35 per cent of the domestic Scotch whisky market and over 50 per cent of the total whisky production in the UK. This would have given the group a dominance of the market not known since the heyday of Distillers in the early 1960s. As the *Financial Times's* Lex columnist puts it, '. . . a malt-monopolist with an unchallengeable share of the blended brands . . . (is) . . . a dram on which the OFT must surely gag?'

The two companies were obviously aware of the danger, and did what they could to allay the fears of a jittery market. They insisted that this was a merger rather than a takeover, and statements were made which were positively miserly with the truth. Roger Seelig, of Morgan Grenfell, commented nonchalantly, 'We clearly would not have embarked on this course without taking full benefit of the informal guidance procedure of the OFT'.

Ernest Saunders approached the issue from a different direction, he said '. . . if you consider the strategic importance of this business and its importance to British exports, I can't imagine any British government will worry about one or two points in the British brand share'. He added that the bid was very unlikely to be referred.

All this was news to the Office of Fair Trading which issued a statement the next day. It read: 'There is no, repeat no, question of any bidder having been told at any time that any bid other than that by Argyll for Distillers would not be referred to the Monopolies and Merger Commission for fuller investigation.'

A copy of this statement was telexed to Jimmy Gulliver, who called a press conference within minutes of Ernest Saunders's statement that the bid was unlikely to be referred. Flourishing the OFT statement, Gulliver began, 'A suggestion was certainly made earlier on by Guinness that it had a nod and a wink from the Office of Fair Trading to say that everything is alright. That is not true.'

The time lag between the Guinness bid and the decision as to whether or not it would be referred was creatively spent by both sides, whose work on what they chose to present as facts and figures—either their own or their adversary's—gave a new dimension to the old adage of there being lies, damned lies and statistics. Towards the end of January, Argyll received a stroke of luck when the full details emerged of Distillers commitment to meet Guinness's costs. There was obviously a leak somewhere in the Distillers camp, and Bill Spengler was angry about rumours of a boardroom split and what he saw as the 'side-issue' of the deal taking attention away from the merits of the Guinness bid.

Mutual vilification did not lessen as January turned to February. On the first day of the month Gulliver warned that up to 1,000 jobs might be lost in Scotland if the Guinness/Distillers merger were to go ahead. The warning was given in a letter to Distillers' shareholders from Argyll, in which the whole credibility—and even the competence—of the Distillers board was attacked. According to the letter, the proposed deal, '. . . has been cobbled together too quickly'.

This was followed up with a personal broadside from Gulliver, 'Right up until 19th January they were spending a great deal of time and money suggesting that their new management team had sorted everything out and they didn't need any outside help. The following day they announced the Guinness deal. You just can't take anything they say seriously anymore'.

Saunders was quick to rebut the suggestion that there might be job losses with a Guinness/Distillers merger; saying 'That's really a scurrilous rumour, which I won't have anything to do with'. But Guinness were to suffer another blow when it was announced that their underwriting arrangement with Distillers—'a side-issue'—was to face an inquiry from the Association of British Insurers. One fund-manager, involved with both companies commented, 'A number of big shareholders have been talking to each other about this and a number of courses of action are being considered. We would like to see the law clarified in the whole area of what boards can spend shareholders money on in the course of defending a bid'.

Many people were worried that Distillers' commitment to Guinness amounted to a 'poison-pill' tactic (i.e. the taking on of a debt to make the company less attractive to a predator), and they were reluctant to see such a move established in the UK. Most people thought that the Distillers action was a *fait accompli* about which they could do little. Jimmy Gulliver did not: on 5th February he issued a writ to nullify the agreement under section 151 of the 1985 Companies Act, which prohibits a company from providing financial assistance for the purchase of its own shares. Argyll also extended its offer for Distillers to 15th February, after receiving acceptances covering 2.95 per cent of the shares by its second closing date. Two days later, Argyll was to launch a much more vigorous offensive.

## First Guinness Bid Referred

On 7th February, in a surprise move, Argyll topped Guinness's £2.2 billion bid with a £2.3 billion bid of its own. Although such a move had been expected, most authorities considered that it would not occur until the OFT had decided the issue of whether or not to refer the Guinness bid to the Monopolies Commission. Argyll's increased offer gave 11 new Argyll ordinary shares, 10 new convertible preference shares and £15 cash for every 10 Distillers shares, valuing each Distillers share at 632p, compared with the Guinness offer of 585p. The increased bid was mainly funded through the issue of more shares, with only £36 million more cash: this took Argyll's total borrowings to date to £636 million. The stock market reacted to the move: Argyll's share price dropped 10p to 338p, Distillers gained 25p to 605p, and Guinness fell by 5p to 287p.

Gulliver's timing was superb. In one move he had regained the initiative which had been effectively lost from the day Guinness had entered the arena. On a more subtle level the increased bid had one eye on the OFT, pressing home a little harder the argument that the Guinness bid should be referred. Before the second Argyll offer, Guinness could always have argued that if they were referred the OFT would be denying Distillers shareholders the opportunity of a better offer. This was no longer the case. There was, of course, the minor risk that if the OFT were to refer Guinness they would be seen to be handing Distillers over to Argyll 'on a plate', something which they would be very reluctant to do. To avoid this, there was a chance that both bids might be frozen. Gulliver took the chance, a calculated risk, and it paid off.

On St. Valentine's Day the hearts of the Guinness board were pierced by something far more barbed than Cupid's arrow; their bid had been referred to the Monopolies and Mergers Commission by Geoffrey Pattie, the industry and technology minister who was acting in place of Paul Channon, the Trade Secretary with Guinness family connections. Mr Pattie said that the Guinness bid raised some serious questions about the impact the combine might have on competition, and that the whole issue deserved further investigation. The decision appeared to give Argyll a clear run in, and certain sections of City opinion held that the battle was all over bar the shouting.

Such feelings did not extend to the camps of Guinness and Distillers, however. When the news was announced the Distillers board issued a holding statement reiterating their view that a merger with Guinness made financial and commercial sense, and promising to make a further statement to shareholders. For its part, Guinness did not follow the usual procedure when a takeover had been referred of allowing the bid to lapse. Saunders was determined to fight but the truth was the Guinness/Distillers merger was in serious trouble. It was effectively stalled. Charles Fraser had warned Ernest Saunders as early as December that a bid for Distillers was bound to be referred. Saunders had replied, 'I'm comfortable on that'. 'But Ernest, it's bound to be'. 'No Charles, we're very comfortable on that'. Fraser had warned Saunders and Ward again on Saturday 11th January when he had met them at the Caledonian. Saunders had said, 'Don't worry. I have very good contacts.'

### Lever and Swift to the Rescue

Now in mid-February, Saunders was in trouble and he telephoned Fraser on Saturday, 15th February to see if he could get him out of it. As it happened Fraser could. In his capacity as deputy chairman of United Biscuits he had been privy to the deal whereby United Biscuits and Imperial had received clearance of their merger by agreeing to sell off certain brands in the snack market if their merger went through.

The two key barristers who had worked on the United Biscuits/Imperial deal were Jeremy Lever, QC and John Swift, QC. Fraser tracked them down that Saturday. Lever was having dinner at All Souls College, Oxford with Lord Hailsham. He listened to Fraser and said, 'Arrange a car to be at my house at 10 o'clock tomorrow morning with all the relevant papers. After I have studied them the chauffeur can then drive me to the Guinness headquarters where I will meet you and Saunders for lunch.'

This was duly arranged, Fraser flew down to London and they all met for lunch. Afterwards they adjourned to the board room where Lever said, 'I'll sit at the head of the table'. He then gave his views, his judgment and his plan whereupon he departed to leave John Swift, also brought in from the country, to put the plan into action. Swift worked for three days and three nights and emerged with the solution.

10.    John Connell, chairman of Distillers. He had been
brought up to expect to be chairman and chairman he was —
for a time.

11.    Alick Rankin, chief
executive of Scottish
and Newcastle
Breweries. He nearly
merged with Distillers.

12. Sir Thomas Risk, Governor of the Bank of Scotland. He did not want to be chairman of Guinness, though having accepted, he was not going back on a commitment. In retrospect he is lucky he never became chairman.

13. Sir Robin Leigh Pemberton, Governor of the Bank of England. Belatedly the Bank insisted on some resignations.

14. Lord Rockley, director of Kleinwort Benson. Better to fall into the arms of Guinness than Argyll — or was it?

15. Sir Nigel Broackes, chairman of Trafalgar House and appointed a director of Distillers. Appointed too late to be effective.

16. Tiny Rowland, chief executive of Lonrho. He walked off with a bargain — 10% of the whisky market for £3½ million. Andrew Alexander of the *Daily Mail* did not like it.

# The Bid for Distillers

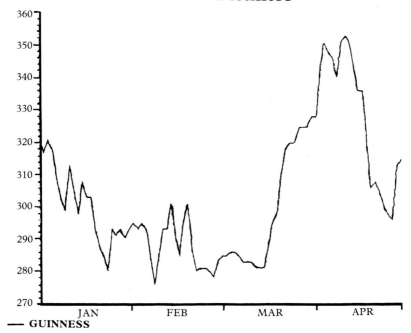

**GUINNESS**

17.  The crucial rise of the Guinness share price from mid March until the success of the bid in mid April.

18.   Tom Ward, American lawyer. Never far from Saunders' elbow, but was he the consilieri or just a 'wee rogue'?

19.  Olivier Roux, a french consultant from Bain and Co. The finance director who claimed he knew little about finance.

20. Sir Norman Macfarlane, chairman, Macfarlane Group. New non-executive director and then chairman at Guinness. Said in August 1986, 'There comes a time when everyone must stop crying foul and get on with the game.' Later he added his voice to those crying foul.

On 20th February, Guinness informed the Commission that it had cancelled its previous bid and was submitting a new offer. Guinness's new bid offered five new Guinness shares and 516p cash for every three Distillers shares, valuing each Distillers share at around 647p and making the whole bid worth £2.34 billion. More importantly, the new offer carried a commitment for the sale of at least five relatively small whisky distilleries (Claymore, with a 6 per cent market share, Haig Gold Label (2.8 per cent), Real Mackenzie (0.8 per cent), Buchanan Blend (0.2 per cent) and John Barr (0.17 per cent)) which would have reduced the Guinness/Distillers share of the UK whisky market to around 25 per cent. Guinness were keen to sell the brands off as a single unit, and Grand Metropolitan and Highland Distilleries were said to be interested. Failing that, Morgan Grenfell were ready to acquire the brands on 'a temporary basis'.

However, the offer was not as seductive as it seemed, and it was no certainty that the OFT would let the bid pass. The divestment of Claymore, a very cheap whisky, and several minor brands was superficially impressive, but it did little to change the overall market share in the areas that mattered. The two companies could only wait and hope. Their spirits could not have been raised by a letter from Lord Spens, a former financial adviser to Bell's during the Guinness takeover, in the *Financial Times* on 21st February. In his letter, Lord Spens attacked Guinness's decision to hive off Bell's Real Mackenzie brand, citing it as one example of promises given by Guinness being 'flagrantly abandoned in the pursuit of naked ambition, and so soon after the event'. In view of events later in the year, it was a fascinating intervention.

If that were not enough, Argyll launched a new offensive through the courts. The company applied for judicial review to block the new Guinness offer on the grounds that it was not fundamentally different from the first bid. Argyll argued that the offer of 20th February was not a 'new bid' within the meaning of the 1973 Fair Trading Act. An Argyll executive explained, 'We want to discover whether the Commission actually realised that when Guinness asked to have its bid laid aside it was going to make a slightly different one later'.

The case went for full judicial review on Thursday 27th February. Argyll still held the initiative: their share price had risen by 9p to 342p and they held some 11.5 per cent of Distillers' shares. Guinness remained steady at 280p, and they and their concert parties could claim an 8 per cent stake in Distillers.

Ernest Saunders retaliated in a novel way. In a press conference he claimed that Argyll's 'diversionary tactic' did not worry him in the slightest and he appealed to Guinness shareholders to write to the OFT, their MP's and even Margaret Thatcher to support the company's bid for Distillers! He then applied for a deferment of the review, via the Treasury Solicitor, to prepare Guinness's defence. This deferment was granted.

The review finally convened in the second week of March 1986, and heard evidence for three days. On the 10th of that month, it handed down its judgment: it dismissed Argyll's case, holding that Sir Godfrey Le Quesne, QC, chairman of the Monopolies Commission, had acted within his powers by deciding personally that Guinness had legally abandoned its original merger proposals. Furthermore, Mr Justice Macpherson added that in his opinion the new Guinness bid was significantly different from the original offer. It would have been too much to expect the last word to be spoken at such a comparatively early stage: Argyll moved the case to the Court of Appeal.

## Dirty Tricks

For those who were beginning to tire of the overly forensic nature of the battle thus far—and there were more court cases to come—March also brought some rather sinister developments. The first development was the revelation that Jimmy Gulliver had been caught out in one of those embarrassing little lies that not only compromised his credibility, but also made him look something of a fool. The lie concerned his entry in *Who's Who* which implied that he had a degree from Harvard University. This had often been mentioned in press articles concerning Gulliver and nobody had bothered to check up on it. After all, why should they? With one of the bitterest takeover battles hotting up by the day, somebody found out why they should. It transpired that James Gulliver's Harvard MBA was in reality a three-week training course at Harvard Business School. Why a man of his undoubted ability and impressive record of achievement should wish to embellish his academic standing is anybody's guess. It was all rather pathetic, but in the hot-house climate of the Guinness/Argyll confrontation, it blossomed out of all proportion. There were calls for Gulliver's resignation. Gulliver himself was deeply hurt and embarrassed by the revelation. Rupert Faure-Walker of Samuel

Montagu remembers it as a thoroughly depressing weekend. Bill Spengler appealed for a return to sane and sensible behaviour in the bid, and categorically asserted that at no time had Distillers sought any information pertaining to Gulliver's private life. Spengler concluded, 'He (Gulliver) doesn't need a bodyguard or anything like that. Distillers is not a company that operates in that way'.

But the rumours continued and the revelations unfolded. In some ways it was like the claim and the counter-claim in the advertising war between the two camps: a mysterious burglary at the home of Distillers director, David Connell met with the suggestion that Jimmy Gulliver's home had also been burgled in recent weeks. It seemed that something more than American financial techniques were coming to these shores.

On 14th March, the struggle returned to the law courts; the Court of Appeal upheld the High Court's decision on Guinness's original bid, and Guinness added to the growing pile of lawsuits when it issued a number of writs against Argyll and its several and various advisers. The writs, alleging 'falsehood and defamation' in advertisements issued by and on behalf of Argyll between 31st January and 12th March 1986, were issued against Argyll, Gulliver, finance director David Webster, merchant bankers Samuel Montagu, Noble Grossart and Charterhouse Japhet, Saatchi and Saatchi and public relations company Broad Street Associates.

The Guinness lawyers, said, 'This action is about advertisements which are regarded as disgraceful. The view is taken that enough is enough. This is bad for the City and you have to call a halt at some stage.' Argyll said that it had no intention of withdrawing the offending advertisements, which they had cleared with their own solicitors and the OFT. Why would one have expected otherwise?

## The Second Bid is Cleared

On March 21st, the Department of Trade and Industry pronounced itself satisfied with Guinness's second bid and announced that it would not be referred. This, of course, was critical and the Argyll camp was ready. Samuel Montagu had prepared a contingency plan. The plan was to increase Argyll's bid and to go into the market and buy no less than 115 million shares at 660p with £700 million—an audacious plan indeed! It is not every day a stockbroker gets an order to buy £700 million worth of one stock.

The £700 million had been raised in 36 hours from Midland Bank and Citicorp. A moment of pure farce entered the proceedings at 114 Old Broad Street when it was realised that it had taken Samuel Montagu only 36 hours to raise £700 million (and less than that to incorporate a company for the transaction) but that it would take six weeks to obtain a machine to apply the company seal to the necessary documents. Nothing if not resourceful, Montagu produced a potato from the kitchen, cut it in half, carved the necessary words (in reverse presumably), dipped the potato in ink and sealed the documents to authorise loans worth £700 milion!

Alas, it was all in vain. As soon as the OFT cleared the Guinness bid, someone started buying Guinness shares and the value of their bid for Distillers rose beyond the price Montagu could pay under the takeover rules. Most observers considered that Guinness had the wherewithal to raise their bid once again, if need be, whilst Argyll had few more shots left in its locker; the campaign was reckoned to be costing them at least £2 million a week, which meant a total cost of some £40 million to date—effectively wiping out a whole year of Argyll's trading. Guinness's costs, which had passed the £40 million mark early in March, were now approaching £60 million, but they had the cushion of their underwriting arrangement with Distillers to fall back on. (We must wonder whether the Distillers board had realised how high the bid costs might rise when they had voted—unanimously—to accept the merger and the costs in January.)

With its share reversal on the stock market, Argyll sought some avenue by which to launch a last minute counter-attack. Once more they found it in the courts, this time under Article 86 of the Treaty of Rome, the EEC statute that was binding on all members of the European Common Market. Article 86 stated that, 'Any abuse of a dominant position within the Common Market . . . shall be prohibited as incompatible with the Common Market in so far as it may affect trade between member states'.

Argyll argued that the combination of Distillers and Guinness whisky brands would indeed be detrimental to both producers and consumers, and might have European repercussions. Guinness were less convinced. A company spokesman retorted, somewhat wearily, 'Coming on the heels of Argyll's failed attempts to block the Guinness bid in the High Court and the Court of Appeal this is just another attempt to remove the decision from Distillers's shareholders'.

On 11th April, a week before the closing date for the rival bids, the

European Commission formally agreed to investigate the implications of a Guinness/Distillers merger. The investigation was expected to take at least six months, and the Commission was empowered to fine the combine—if it materialised—up to 10 per cent of annual profits should there be any infringement of Article 86. That was a prospect Guinness would face if and when it arrived.

In the meantime, Guinness was forging ahead in the battle for Distillers. On 8th April they claimed new acceptances of 9 per cent of Distillers's shareholders to add to the 10.5 per cent they already had. Argyll could only muster 2.5 per cent to add to its existing 14.5 per cent stake. The next day, Bill Spengler announced that Distillers had contacted over 7,000 small shareholders to gain some idea of how they would vote. A majority of 17 to 1 favoured the Guinness bid over Argyll's.

As we know now, there were moves afoot throughout the world to boost the Guinness share price and thus increase the value of their bid.

As the battle entered its final week, the bookmakers were making Guinness 6–4 odds on favourites. They had amassed a 19.5 per cent acceptance stake in Distillers compared with Argyll's 17.5 per cent, and fluctuations in Argyll's share price made Guinness's offer worth 776p against Argyll's 762p.

Wednesday, 16th April was an absolutely critical day in that final week. Warburg Investment Management were prepared to sell 10 million Distillers shares. When the jobber offered them to Montagu they said they would buy at 660p—the most they were allowed to pay. Guinness were only allowed to pay 630p and Montagu felt confident they would get the block. They were therefore utterly devastated to hear that Cazenove, the broker acting for Guinness, had bought them at 700p. They immediately asked the Takeover Panel to investigate but at that moment the Argyll camp knew it was all over. Jimmy Gulliver told Faure-Walker exactly that when Faure-Walker telephoned to give him the news. And they were right. The news quickly spread. The bandwagon effect started to roll and when judgment day arrived on Friday, 18th April, Guinness claimed victory.

### 'The Toucan has Landed!'

Thus was the news of Guinness's victory heralded in the *Financial Times* of Saturday, 19th April. The £2.5 billion bid was finally secured just before 1 p.m. on Friday, when Guinness declared its offer to be unconditional and announced that it had acquired the use of 50.74 per cent of Distillers shares. Argyll conceded defeat at once, and said that it would accept Guinness's offer for its own stake. As trading closed, Guinness had received acceptances from the holders of almost 80 per cent of Distillers shares although the Prudential went to Argyll. John Connell announced that, 'The creation of a British-owned drinks company of this truly international scale is a momentous event. In harness with Guinness we can now look forward to a future which is brighter with promise for our brands, for our business and for Scotland.'

Both parties accepted the result with a charm that belied the bitterness of the campaign that had gone before: both planned parties for that night, and Guinness was as gracious in victory as Argyll was in defeat. (Gulliver wrote a personal note to Saunders congratulating him). Without any doubt, Ernest Saunders had every reason to be a very happy man that weekend: not even the defeat of Queens Park Rangers (sponsored by Guinness) by Oxford in the Milk Cup final on the Sunday could spoil his moment of glory. And with his establishment as the rising star in the British business firmament one might ask if anything could stop him.

# FIVE

## The Thomas Risk Affair

To Arthur Guinness and sons with *ceud mile failte* (a hundred thousand welcomes).

### Exordium (Summary)

The Bank is but the Guinness stamp. The Scots are *cuifs* (disagreeable nitwits) for a 'that'.

### Discussion

When Greeks and Romans ruled the land
They often failed to understand
The sharp and sudden strokes of fate
Which brought disaster on the State.
So oracles were asked their view
On what was what and what to do.
In Scotland surely time has come

To imitate old Greece and Rome
And hear what native Sybils* think
On prospects for our Scottish drink.
Let's state the problem for the seer
And listen for her answer dear.


## The Question Posed

Must Irish cunning still prevail,
Must Scottish hopes forever fail?
Are all our boasted banking skills
Incapable of running stills?
Or can we muster courage yet
And so repel the Thenian threat?
Surely we can . . . oh hear our prayer
And teach us once again to dare.


## The Sybil Speaks

Scotsmen despair! No hope remains
Your spirits lie in servile chains.
The pass has been naively sold
To traffickers in fairy gold.
Your country's birthright pawned alas
For Irish blarney, Irish brass.
So simple-minded Scots are conned
An Irish word's an Irish bond
The wasted effort to reclaim
The brands that made Distillers name.
The Haig, the Dewars, the Black and White,
John Begg and all the labels bright
That glorified identic blends
And shared the snobs with choice of trends.
All—all is lost! So bend the knee
And love that Irish barley bree!


*Sybils gave prophesies with foaming mouths.

The Thomas Risk Affair

## No Way Out?

But what of promises declared
That management would all be shared,
A Scottish chairman with control
In Scotland centred and the whole
Administration pledged to stand
In premises on Scottish land?

## Again the Sybil

A Shunkie* in the walk of Leith
A bonded warehouse in Dalkeith
Will symbolise the Guinness reign,
And leave their honour free from stain.
The Board? When Saunders thought it risky
To put a Scot too close to whisky
He soon found ways to play the pliskie.†
He saw that there was room to live
With posts called "non-exec"
No toos and fros, no toos and froms
Find me some Scottish Uncle Toms.

## Scotland's Last Appeal

O Sybil speak some mercy show
Give us of hope some gleam or glow.

## The Sybil's Message

You want my answer yet again!
I'll riddle in true delphic strain.
When Guinness turns blue or gray
When Paisley joins the IRA
When Rose Street taverns shut their doors
Against the clergy and the whores
When Arthur sits on Arthur's seat
And Princes piss in Princes Street,

*Outside lavatory
†Dirty trick

Then shall the realm of Albion
Emerge from great confusion.
Then shall old Scotland rise anew
But—till my riddles all come true
Guinness is good for cuifs like you!

### Apodectic

Burns said (tho aft inclined to blether)
'Freedom and whisky gang the gither'
So noo yez kens whit Rabbie meant
Wur freedom's gone, wur whisky's went!

Reproduced by courtesy of Sir Andrew Gilchrist.

## Tom Risk—The Man

Contrary to the image that some were keen to portray throughout the summer of 1986, Sir Thomas Risk is not a doddering old Scot who somehow reached the top in the Bank of Scotland through family or 'old boy' connections. Risk, born on 13th September 1922, was educated at Kelvinside Academy and Glasgow University and during the war served in the RAF as a flying boat pilot. After the War he joined a firm of solicitors, Maclay, Murray and Spens in Glasgow and became a partner in 1950. He became a director of the Standard Life Assurance Society (Europe's largest mutual life assurance society) in 1965 and was appointed chairman in 1969, a position he held until 1977. He became a director of British Linen Bank, merchant banking subsidiary of Bank of Scotland in 1968 and was its Governor until 1986. He is also a director of several other public companies including, since 1983, Shell UK Limited. He became a director of Bank of Scotland in 1971, Deputy Governor in 1977 and Governor in 1981.

But if the Guinness public relations machine conveyed a false impression, the unbiased media also portrayed him wrongly using words like 'patrician' and emphasising the 'Sir Thomas'. In fact, Tom Risk, as he is known and likes to be known, does not have a patrician background. His father, also a lawyer, had strong Glasgow roots and in his younger days played football for the famous amateur club, Queens Park at Hampden Park. Risk himself, as his friend at Maclay, Murray and Spens, Tom Laurie, points out, knows his way round the Glasgow sheriff's court.

Risk is however a man of high principles and integrity. Furthermore, and this is critical in the story of his on-off chairmanship of Guinness, he is a man who likes to know what is going on in any situation where he has any responsibility. He is also, of course, a Scot.

It was Risk's commitment to the success of Scotland that finally persuaded him to agree to serve as chairman of Guinness when he was urged to do so in January 1986. It was put to him, forcefully, that by doing so he would be helping to revive the flagging Scottish company Distillers, in a flagging industry, the distilling and marketing of Scotch whisky. He had watched many Scottish industries and companies decline and even disappear during his business life and he was one of those in Scotland determined to reverse this trend.

This commitment to Scotland outweighed Risk's misgivings about the appropriateness of the Governor of the Bank of Scotland becoming involved in what might prove to be a bitterly fought triangular takeover battle. He accepted the fact that he was becoming an ally of what might be seen as the English (with perhaps a touch of the Irish) side against the apparently 100 per cent Scottish Argyll Group. He dismissed the idea as ridiculous, that his agreeing to make himself available could be criticised when it came so soon after Distillers had transferred some of their banking business from Royal Bank to Bank of Scotland. The two things were quite unconnected in his mind and he said so at the time. (John Connell, prompted by advisers in Edinburgh, had finally made the transfer in December 1985 when it was discovered that the Royal Bank, through its subsidiary, Charterhouse Japhet, was providing part of the £600 million loan to help Jimmy Gulliver's Argyll Group take over Distillers.)

If Distillers were determined to change their bankers it was understandable Bank of Scotland would hope to inherit the business. They already handled the accounts of some of the subsidiaries. Some, however, felt it was going a little far for the Governor to accept the office of the chair within a month of the transfer of the accounts. .

Alick Rankin, chief executive of Scottish and Newcastle Breweries, certainly did not like it and rang Bruce Pattullo, the treasurer (general manager) and told him so.

Angus Grossart did not like it either and referred to Fraser and Risk as the 'rent-a-kilt' brigade (*The Scotsman* surprisingly could not follow the wit and printed it, twice in the same article, as 'Rentokil'). Grossart would of course not like it because as an adviser to Gulliver he could see what a master-stroke it was by Guinness.

## The Decision to Ask Tom Risk

There is even some controversy over how Risk came to be asked to be chairman in the first place and there are differing versions of what happened. Ivan Fallon, writing in the *Sunday Times* on 14th September 1986, said that Risk was pushed forward by Charles Fraser after Guinness and Distillers had agreed the general terms of the 'merger' over the weekend of 18th/19th January 1986. According to Fallon, Bay Green of Kleinwort Benson (Distillers' advisers) and Roger Seelig of Morgan Grenfell (Guinness' advisers) met to agree the final details. One of the details was—who should be chairman? Apparently both Lord Iveagh, the Guinness chairman, and John Connell, the Distillers chairman, wanted to head the combined group. However, Lord Iveagh soon realised he was not acceptable to the Scots, and the Guinness camp were certainly not having John Connell. Connell had after all presided over Distillers as its overall performance continued to decline and as it became ever more vulnerable to a predator whether it be Argyll or Guinness.

According to Fallon, Risk was available, Charles Fraser pushed him forward and Ernest Saunders raised no objection. Saunders said he had met Risk but barely knew him.

What actually happened on that crucial weekend from 17th January to 19th January was this. On the Friday Risk, on his way to the Bank of Scotland's chief office in London, was telephoned by Saunders and invited to meet Saunders and Roger Seelig on an 'urgent matter' at Guinness's office in Portman Square. He agreed to do so. He was then told of the plans for an agreed merger between Guinness and Distillers and was asked if he would be prepared to accept the invitation of both boards, which was endorsed by their respective merchant bank advisers, to become chairman of the new group.

Risk's immediate reaction was to reject the proposal out of hand. He had a full-time job as Governor of the Bank of Scotland and had no wish to take on any new commitments. At this point Saunders used all his persuasiveness to try to make Risk change his mind. He expounded on the need for Distillers to be revived, to market its wares successfully on an international basis but also to become again fully involved in the Scottish community. This need for involvement in Scotland had already been made a major issue by Gulliver and it was clear that Saunders recognised the appeal that this had had for many influential people whose support the proposed Guinness/Distillers merger would require.

Risk decided that the proposal was one of such importance that he must consider it very seriously and that he must consult his board and senior management colleagues at the bank. Saunders explained that the timetable was very tight, the press were already suspicious and an announcement might have to be made first thing on Monday morning. He asked for a decision over the weekend, which Risk agreed to give. During the next 24 hours Risk succeeded in contacting most of his colleagues and, as a result of these consultations, he decided, rather reluctantly, that it was his duty to accept nomination as prospective chairman of the board of the new merged company. He had flown back to Edinburgh on Friday evening and telephoned Saunders from his home on the Saturday. There were to be further negotiations between Distillers and Guinness on the Sunday in London and Risk flew down again in case he was needed. In the event, apart from a meeting with Distillers' merchant bankers who confirmed that it was their wish and that of the Distillers board that he should accept the appointment of chairman, he was not required.

Charles Fraser was not at any of these meetings. Indeed that particular weekend he was at his house in Inverness. Saunders was in touch with him by telephone—Fraser was after all chairman of Morgan Grenfell (Scotland)—and eventually reported that Risk had agreed to become chairman. Fraser was naturally delighted. This version is an accurate version of what happened but of course it sheds no light on who suggested Risk.

Another version of events, and a view held by many of the Edinburgh financial community including Ray Perman, the editor of the up and coming Scottish business monthly *Scottish Business Insider* is that Charles Fraser wittingly or unwittingly engineered the appointment of Sir Thomas Risk even if he did not actually suggest it. Remember that John Connell had taken the Distillers account away from the Royal Bank and placed it with the Bank of Scotland. After that it might have been thought that Bank of Scotland would have been bound at all costs to help Distillers escape the clutches of Argyll. Risk did not feel any such obligation and made his feelings quite clear to John Connell. However, when Distillers' chosen course was to embrace Guinness, what better choice could there be as the independent and Scottish chairman than someone who, as well as his other qualifications, held the office of Governor of Bank of Scotland?

The truth is probably a combination of these versions. Although the official line disseminated by Guinness in January 1986 was that

Distillers had turned to them in distress, in fact Guinness had been preparing the ground to bid for Distillers in the autumn of 1985. They were alarmed, having just bought Bell's, at the prospect of Distillers' famous brands being aggressively marketed by the dynamic Argyll Group. Sir Nigel Broackes remembers being told by John Connell that Distillers had considered bidding for Guinness in the summer of 1985. (The Distillers board considered many things. Unfortunately it did not seem to do many of them.)

In the autumn of 1985 Charles Fraser was consulted by Saunders. Indeed he had advised him on the takeover of Bell's and was on the Bell's board (although in true Saunders fashion it was a board that never seemed to meet.) Fraser attended meetings of the Guinness team in December 1985 which were discussing the takeover of Distillers. What more sensible arrangement could there have been than for the dynamic marketing man, Saunders, to be chief executive, and the Scotsman and man of integrity, Sir Thomas Risk, to be chairman? Whoever thought of it, it was a stroke of pure genius. And for the moment it satisfied all parties.

## The Bombshell of Sunday 13th July

On Sunday 13th July, Ivan Fallon in the *Sunday Times* printed the story, carefully leaked by Guinness, that Risk was not after all going to be chairman of the Guinness/Distillers group. This was followed by an article by Kenneth Fleet in *The Times* on the Monday which included the following statement, 'The most controversial departure is likely to be that of Sir Thomas Risk, Governor of the Bank of Scotland and a "name" trumpetted by Guinness during the takeover battle when Mr James Gulliver and Argyll stood at a heavy premium in Scottishness. It appears that the Bank of Scotland through its Governor, is demanding more of the Group's banking business than the Guinness board believes is justified. Furthermore, friction between Mr Ernest Saunders and Sir Thomas has been increased by Sir Thomas's insistence on the role of "Scotland's voice" in the planning and decision-making which will reshape and streamline Distillers' operations. The urgency of dealing with Distillers' deeply etched problems and the need to show that the grass is not growing under Mr Saunders' feet have persuaded the Guinness board that there should be a single high command structure.'

It was generous of Fleet to talk of the Guinness board making decisions. By the summer of 1986 Saunders was hardly consulting his board. Indeed he had boasted to an American financier that he did not even consult them before making the bid for Distillers. In the spring, Viscount Boyd of Merton had resigned from the board, apparently because major events were occurring without his knowledge.

In fact, Risk, far from 'demanding more of the group's business' had actually made it clear to Saunders that where the company's banking business was placed was a question on which possible conflicts of interest would mean that he, as chairman, could and would take no part. Secondly, how could friction between Saunders and Sir Thomas have been 'increased by Sir Thomas's insistence on the role of "Scotland's voice" in the planning and decision making' when (as we shall see in a minute) at the first meeting the two men had after the success of the takeover, Saunders told Risk that he was not going to be chairman. Thirdly, if Kenneth Fleet seriously thought that Guinness had suddenly discovered after April 1986 that the problems of Distillers were so immense that there was no room for a chairman as well as a chief executive, he was not being very perceptive. There were some who might have argued that if the problems of Distillers were so appalling that was all the more reason for having a separate chairman so that the chief executive could concentrate single-mindedly on sorting them out.

All hell broke loose on the Sunday and Monday. Here was a test for the 'new' City. A major company was reneging on a promise made in a 'takeover document' sent to shareholders in the middle of a takeover battle. As Charles Fraser said, 'Undertakings were given to Sir Thomas Risk and myself before the campaign began. But undertakings to two individuals are of much less consequence than undertakings in Offer Documents accepted by all Distillers shareholders. It speaks for itself'.

There was no question about it, all the takeover documents from the first press release announcing the merger to the formal Offer Documents issued by Guinness on 3rd March 1986 stated categorically to Distillers shareholders that 'following the merger, Sir Thomas Risk, Governor of the Bank of Scotland, will be appointed non-executive chairman of the combined group'.

Most people took the view that such an undertaking was sacrosanct, indeed that it was legally binding. Guinness, a company that had received much legal advice in the previous 12 months, and which had an American lawyer, Tom Ward, sitting at Saunders' right elbow,

throughout took the view that promises made in takeover documents were neither sacrosanct nor legally binding. Incredibly, as we shall see, the Bank of England, the Stock Exchange, and most financial institutions in the end seem to have accepted that view.

## Men of Principle Become Men of Straw

Initially there were shouts of 'foul' on all sides. The revelations were of course not new to a coterie of advisers. Morgan Grenfell and Cazenove had known of Saunders' intentions to ditch Risk for some time. Indeed, Risk and Fraser had attended meetings to discuss this very matter.

Risk, after his difficult meeting with Saunders and Ward in Washington in mid-May, had had only one other meeting with Saunders. That meeting had been at the Savoy hotel where the two had met for dinner on Thursday, 26th June. Risk remembers that the dinner was not in any way acrimonious but that he emphasised repeatedly to Saunders the potentially calamitous consequences for the Guinness board of their failing to deliver on promises made in the takeover documents. Saunders said he would reconsider but was finding it difficult to get Lord Iveagh and the Guinness family to agree. In the course of the discussion Saunders asked Risk how he saw the banking arrangements for the new group. Risk replied that as chairman of the company, and also of its principal bankers, he could not possibly seek to influence decisions which would have to be made by the executive with board approval. He hoped, of course, that the Bank of Scotland would continue to have a share of the new group's banking business but if they did so it would have to be because they were competitive in price and standard of service. As we now know, this was reported as, 'The Bank of Scotland through its Governor, is demanding more of the group's banking business than the Guinness board believes is justified' (Kenneth Fleet in *The Times*, Monday 14th July 1986).

Following this second meeting between Risk and Saunders, events moved quickly. Morgan Grenfell and Cazenove were privy to the problems but Wood Mackenzie, Guinness' other stockbroker, indeed theoretically their lead broker, were not. This in itself was strange, but we will come back to that. When Chiene learnt he was outraged and demanded an immediate meeting of all the parties concerned. On Thursday 10th July at Morgan Grenfell's offices the advisers assembled—Morgan Grenfell, Cazenove, Kleinwort Benson and Wood Mackenzie. Risk and Fraser were also present.

Christopher Reeves, the chief executive of Morgan Grenfell, played the ambassadorial role trying to seek an acceptable compromise. John Chiene was having none of that. He insisted that unless undertakings given in a takeover document were adhered to then they must all resign. And that was the agreement—unless Saunders changed his mind they would all resign. John Chiene then sought a meeting with Guinness and he and a colleague, Scott Dobie, met Tom Ward. Ward told them how impossible Tom Risk was and that they could not work with him. John Chiene knew Tom Risk and knew better but kept his own counsel. On Friday 11th July, Chiene spent an hour and a quarter with Ernest Saunders and Lord Iveagh and even told them that Risk had offered to stand down if they could find a substitute who was acceptable to both Guinness and Risk. But an independent and non-executive chairman was necessary. It had been promised. This was not acceptable to Saunders and he walked out of the meeting without even saying goodbye to John Chiene. It was left to Lord Iveagh, to maintain at least a facade of civilised behaviour. He and Chiene agreed that nothing should be made public until further attempts at a solution had been tried.

But the Guinness side decided they had had enough of meetings to discuss a matter they had already decided and on Sunday 13th July Ivan Fallon writing in the *Sunday Times,* produced his 'Saunders needs an unfettered hand' article. As it happened John Chiene was queuing in his car to get into Brands Hatch to watch the British grand prix when his car telephone rang and a colleague asked him if he had seen the *Sunday Times.* He had not and had to borrow one from the man in the car behind (if a motor racing enthusiast remembers lending the *Sunday Times* to a tall, distinguished Scot, that was John Chiene about to resign from being Guinness' stockbroker).

At this stage perhaps, we should look at John Chiene's and Wood Mackenzie's role in the whole affair. John Chiene is often called Johnny Chiene to distinguish him from his father John Chiene who was closely involved in the Edinburgh financial community from the 1930s to the 1970s. (Interestingly, he also ran Robert Brown who made the exclusive Chivas Regal whisky, later to be taken over by Seagrams.) Johnny has brought Wood Mackenzie, which he joined in 1962, from a firm employing nine people in Edinburgh with no institutional clients to the Wood Mackenzie of today, one of London's leading stockbrokers, renowned for its analytical research. It is now part of Hill Samuel and John Chiene has recently been appointed joint chief executive and head of investment banking at Hill Samuel and Co. John is a Scot but he realised long ago that the main financial market in the United Kingdom was London.

Wood Mackenzie's involvement with Guinness began soon after Saunders' appointment as managing director. One of the first actions taken by Saunders was to collate all the research done by brokers on the company. He noticed that almost alone Wood Mackenzie had produced an in-depth analysis and had criticised the Guinness attempts at diversification. In short, the report had said Guinness was a shambles. Saunders agreed with that.

Saunders consequently formed a relationship with Scott Dobie of Wood Mackenzie and eventually replaced James Capel with Wood Mackenzie as the company's broker. One of Wood Mackenzie's first tasks was to underwrite Guinness' offer for Martins the newsagents in 1984. At this stage the Wood Mackenzie team were very impressed with Ernest Saunders as he cleaned out the Augean stables even if he did not quite equal Hercules' task of doing it in one day. Saunders was also beginning to re-establish the Guinness brands.

By early 1985 Saunders was ready (after the series of smaller takeovers) to consider the much bigger prize of Bell's, but in the meantime John Chiene had been asked by Jimmy Gulliver if Wood Mackenzie would act as consultants as he looked at the possibility of bidding for Distillers. As far as John Chiene was concerned it was clear, though never formally agreed, that Wood Mackenzie would act for Argyll in the event of a bid for Distillers. When Chiene learnt of Guinness' plans to bid for Bell's he said to Gulliver, 'We must hurry up and finish your research because we have another client who may be about to get involved in the whisky business'.

Jimmy Gulliver was apparently understanding about this. As we have already seen, Guinness bid for Bell's and won the ensuing battle easily.

Wood Mackenzie continued as Guinness' main stockbroker and on Friday, 17th January 1986 John Chiene was summoned to the offices of Morgan Grenfell and told that Guinness was going to bid for (i.e. merge with) Distillers. Chiene was concerned because of their involvement a year earlier in carrying out research for Argyll on Distillers. However, he discussed it with Jimmy Gulliver, who again accepted the situation with good grace, and John Chiene agreed that Wood Mackenzie would act for Guinness provided that the three who had carried out the research, himself, Philip Augar and Ian McBeen were not involved.

Chiene was both surprised and hurt that Morgan Grenfell told him that Cazenove would be the broker buying shares in the market. His protests were brushed aside by Roger Seelig with the comment, 'It's not available for discussion'.

It was Wood Mackenzie who bought a part of the famous Schenley stake on behalf of a leading US securities house. At the time they asked if the stake was for someone with associate status with Guinness. They were assured it was not. The stock was ultimately registered in the name of Atlantic Nominees. Eventually, of course, Guinness was successful in the takeover and although he went to the victory party, Chiene felt that there was a sudden silence on specific details about how the new company was going to operate. A presentation in New York in May to which John Chiene had been invited was long on 'ra ra' but short on actual plans.

Then, out of the blue, came the call from Charles Fraser that Risk was not to be chairman. Chiene was shocked and appalled and never once changed his stance—either Sir Thomas Risk was to become chairman or Wood Mackenzie would resign. As the drama unfolded on Monday 14th and Tuesday 15th July and others such as Morgan Grenfell and Cazenove confined themselves to pompous noises about compromise, Wood Mackenzie resigned. They were conspicuously alone in doing so, although Charles Fraser publicly declared that he was no longer available to serve on the Guinness board, his law firm seized to act for Guinness and subsequently he resigned from Morgan Grenfell.

Apart from Alf Young in the *Scotsman* and Hamish McRae in the *Guardian* few seemed to support the Fraser/Wood Mackenzie stand. Kenneth Fleet wrote in *The Times*, 'If Distillers' directors, Scottish sympathisers and City of London advisers believed that Guinness had done its duty when, with their active support, Guinness had rid them of the pesky Jimmy Gulliver, they clearly had a shock coming to them. The "Scottish dimension" is misty and powerful and needs to be carefully watched. Even plainer, Distillers needs strong management and a massive dose of constructive interference. It was not likely to get it with a "balanced" board. From the point of view of the City, and the Bank of England, the situation created by the latest Guinness moves is serious but hardly critical'.

Morgan Grenfell and Cazenove persuaded Saunders to put the new proposed board structure to the shareholders. As we shall see, the Bank of England, the Stock Exchange and the Takeover Panel huffed and puffed a bit but effectively in the end did nothing. There was one moment of farce when the Bank of England, having requested a visit from the chairman of the Guinness company, received Ernest Saunders instead of the expected Lord Iveagh. (In the time between the request and the appointment Saunders had leaked and then announced that Iveagh was to be president and he was to be the chairman.) We can imagine that in future the Bank will ask for people by name not title. Lex in the *Financial Times* was forthright, 'Having a passing knowledge of acquisition accounting, Mr Ernest Saunders should know all about goodwill. But it will be a long time before anyone loses such accumulated City goodwill in the space of a day as Mr Saunders has achieved by a shameless divergence from the terms of the "merger" with Distillers. . . . What must be explained in detail, before the proposed extraordinary meeting, is the reason for Guinness' swerve away from the policy to which it committed itself in the first explicit documentary way. The reasons given hitherto are vague to the point of being an insult.'

## The Authorities Apply Pressure

Much was made of the pressure brought to bear on Ernest Saunders by the Department of Trade, the Bank of England, the Stock Exchange and the Takeover Panel. If this was so, either Saunders was very good at resisting it or it was being applied in the wrong place in the wrong way. The fact is, Saunders was tearing up an undertaking given to shareholders in a takeover situation. What was at stake was not the more or less efficient running of a drinks company but rather the whole basis of statements and commitments made to shareholders in a takeover situation. No one put it better than Hamish McRae in the *Guardian*, 'The principle should be simple enough. If you say in an offer document that you plan to do certain things with a company should you take it over, then under the present way the country operates you are surely obliged to carry these out. You have to make this point absolutely clear both for practical and for moral reasons. The practical issue is that if you do not accept this principle the offer document in a takeover bid would become wholly worthless. Shareholders would be forced to make up their minds as to the relative merits on the basis of information to which they could attach no credibility whatsoever, and the present basis on which bids are conducted would fall to bits.'

But the authorities did not insist that Guinness keep their promises made to shareholders, and by failing to do so they made sure that in any future contested takeover any statement made will not carry the weight it would have done before July 1986. All the authorities did was to insist on an extraordinary general meeting of the Guinness shareholders at which the new proposals would be voted on. There had to be a circular before this meeting and the authorities cast their eye over this document. As we shall see their attention was little more than perfunctory. Ernest Saunders was also required to appoint five non-executive directors in whom would be vested the power to remove him.

## The Non-Executive Directors

In the event, in spite of reports in the press that Saunders was 'flooded with offers to help' (Kenneth Fleet in *The Times*) and 'flooded with inquiries from banks offering independent advice, brokers ambitious to replace Wood Mackenzie and people who would like to help as directors' (Kenneth Fleet again), Saunders did not find it easy to find five non-executive directors of sufficient standing. Many in Scotland were asked and many declined. Angus Grossart was drafted in to work with Lazards, the Department of Trade and the Scottish Office and Tom Ward to find suitable candidates. (You might ask why Grossart, so unhappy about Guinness' tactics in the recent battle was prepared to do this. His answer is that you have to keep talking to the supposed 'enemy' otherwise open war is inevitable. Ignore Guinness completely and the effect on jobs in Scotland could be damaging.) Many were suggested as candidates—ex MPs, Lords etc.—and eventually some were chosen and approached. By the middle of August four had accepted the invitation and had themselves been accepted by the Bank of England, the Department of Trade and Industry and the Stock Exchange. They were Sir Norman Macfarlane, Sir David Plaistow, Mr Ian MacLaurin and Mr Anthony Greener.

Sir Norman Macfarlane, aged 60, was chairman of the publicly-quoted plastics and packaging concern Macfarlane Group (Clansman). The company, with a turnover approaching £50 million, was already a big supplier to the Distillers group both with bottle closures and labels. A keen cricketer until a few years ago, Sir Norman was described as 'totally clean' and 'integrity personified'. Fraser and Risk are both friends of Sir Norman but perhaps surprisingly he does not appear to have talked to them or told them of his decision.

Sir David Plaistow was the chairman of Vickers. The official line was that his experience in marketing Rolls Royce would be of assistance. Mr Ian MacLaurin was chairman of Tesco and was conscripted for his retail and brand experience (needless to say there was some sour comment from rival supermarket chains about clashes of interest). Mr Anthony Greener was managing director of Dunhill and was felt to be the man responsible for that company's recent growth through the development of their premium brands.

The total number of board members now proposed was 15 and some felt it was as unwieldy as the original board proposed at the time of the takeover. That board would have had four representatives from the old Distillers company—John Connell, David Connell, Bill Spengler and Sir Nigel Broackes—and of course two independent Scottish representatives, Fraser and Risk. The board now proposed had no representatives from Distillers and certainly not Fraser or Risk.

## The Guinness Public Relations Machine Rolls

During July and August the Guinness camp were giving the impression that Sir Thomas Risk was impossible to work with. It was said that he and Ernest Saunders were incompatible. To those who knew Risk and who knew the facts this was all palpable nonsense. But few people outside Scotland and the City did know Risk and fewer still knew the facts. Fact number one was that Ernest Saunders told Risk at their very first business meeting after the Distillers takeover that he did not want him as chairman. If their styles had become incompatible it must have happened very quickly. This meeting had taken place in Washington on Sunday, 18th May.

It is surprising that this was their first meeting since the victory announced on 18th April. The original plan had been for Saunders and Risk to have a weekend together in New York to discuss future strategy. This was changed at the last minute and Risk was asked to come to Washington instead. He flew out on Concorde on the Saturday morning and was told that Saunders was tied up and would see him tomorrow, Sunday. On the Saturday evening Risk had dinner with Vic Steel, managing director of Guinness Brewing Worldwide at the hotel where Risk was staying, the Ritz Carlton. Risk described the conversation as essentially restricted to social matters. Risk eventually saw Saunders and Tom Ward the next day, when they came to his hotel room, and was told that Saunders wanted an executive chairman. Thus, by the time of their very first meeting only four weeks after the takeover of Distillers, Saunders had already decided that promises made in the course of the takeover were not important.

It is critical, in view of what was said by the Guinness camp later, about Risk thumping the table and demanding this and demanding that, to establish whether such a discussion of how Guinness was to be run did take place before Saunders and Ward told Risk they did not want him as chairman.

Apart from the fact that no one who knows him can remember Risk adopting the table-thumping style, it is clear what Saunders and Ward had in mind from Ward's opening remark, 'How do you see your role as chairman, Tom?' Risk then told them how he saw his role as a non-executive chairman which was to support the executive in solving the problems that existed within Distillers and merging the companies together. (Hardly table-thumping and certainly not the defence of Scottish interests at all costs, which was another of the Guinness machine's stories about Risk's attitude.)

But Saunders and Ward were not to be deflected. They expounded on the horrendous problems that they had found in Distillers (in that case they had found them very quickly—it was barely a month since they had been celebrating the capture of this company with its unlocked treasures). Under the circumstances, they told Risk, they did not want him as chairman, but would have Saunders instead.

Risk's reaction was to tell them they were being 'daft' but that they should not rely on his view alone but to go and talk to their advisers. The three went down to lunch in the hotel continuing their discussion. During lunch Ward put forward as a possible solution to the problem the idea that Risk could voluntarily stand down in favour of Saunders using the justification that the problems of the company were such that it needed Saunders as both chairman and chief executive. Risk replied that he had no intention of standing down from a commitment he had made and which had been considered of vital importance by many Distillers shareholders.

In the later discussions with Morgan Grenfell, Risk realised the type of men he was dealing with when he heard from them reports of the conversations he was supposed to have had with Saunders and Ward in Washington. Stories of table-thumping and Scotland's interests above all came back across the Atlantic almost as fast as he did. (In view of the mind-boggling fees and pay-offs that have come to light, it is perhaps instructive to note that Risk paid for this trip to Washington out of his own pocket.)

Sir Nigel Broackes, still at this time a non-executive director of Distillers and also a proposed non-executive of the new, yet-to-be-formed, Guinness board, confirmed that at a meeting with Saunders and Tom Ward on 7th May, i.e. 11 days before Risk's meeting with Saunders in Washington, Tom Ward had said to him, 'When do you think Ernest can become chairman?'. Furthermore, Saunders had said to John Connell only the day after the Distillers victory (when telling him he was no longer to have any executive capacity in reply to Connell's question that he presumed he would remain as non-executive vice chairman to Risk) 'I'm not sure Risk is going to be chairman'.

Jimmy Gammell, former chairman of Ivory and Sime, and a director of both the Bank of Scotland and Standard Life, had also been shocked by Saunders' behaviour. At a dinner given by Risk at the Bank of Scotland flat to introduce some of the Guinness executives to people in the Edinburgh financial community in February 1986, Saunders had lent across the table in the middle of dinner and said to Oliver Roux, 'That board meeting we have next week, it's a nuisance. Cancel it, will you.'

## The Move to Edinburgh

Another promise made at the time of the fight for Distillers was that the Guinness/Distillers group headquarters would be moved to Scotland. In the letter sent to shareholders on 3rd March Saunders said, 'We shall take the necessary steps to make the holding company a Scottish registered company and will move the group headquarters to Edinburgh where the group chief executive's office will be located'.

According to Alf Young of the *Scotsman*, Saunders had told him a few days before he had won the battle for Distillers, 'If we win on Friday, then on Monday we'll be here. I'll be here and so will my key people'. Carole Saunders was photographed ostentatiously looking at houses in Edinburgh New Town, a fashionable area of Edinburgh. Strange then that when Jimmy Gulliver met Carole Saunders at a party a few weeks after the battle and asked her how the house hunting was going, she said, 'Oh, we're looking in Oxfordshire'.

By June it was becoming obvious that this promise was not going to be kept and there were certainly not going to be transfers of key people from London to Edinburgh. Saunders by now was saying that the location of the head office was of secondary importance to getting the problems of Distillers sorted out. Tom Ward was saying that Ernest Saunders would have several offices and that most of them would be where the markets were. This was all very pragmatic. The fact is that in the formal offer documents during the takeover battle Guinness had felt it advisable, even necessary, to say that the group headquarters would be in Scotland.

Several people then, some of them in important and influential positions, were noticing throughout the summer of 1986 that there were several reasons to doubt that Saunders was a man of his word.

## The Doubts Grow

After the success of the bid, Saunders was in New York making a presentation to the investment community, one of whom was friendly with Charles Fraser. Thanking Saunders for an interesting presentation the American asked him to give his regards to Fraser at the next board meeting. The American was left with the distinct impression that Guinness board meetings were few and far between, that they were not seen by Saunders as a routine method of monitoring management performance, but rather that directors were people who were useful to Saunders as and when he required them. The American warned Fraser of the obvious dangers of such a set up.

There were those who were already speculating that the Guinness board was perhaps not meeting as regularly as it should have been, and that the directors were perhaps not receiving all the information that was customary. How often for example did the Bell's board meet after the Guinness takeover? Sir Nigel Broackes was also beginning to wonder. Sir Nigel had joined the Distillers board the day before Jimmy Gulliver launched his bid on 3rd December. He had been asked by Lord Rockley of Kleinwort Benson and though not enthusiastic had agreed as he felt he owed Kleinwort Benson a favour.

Sir Nigel is a very sophisticated and experienced businessman who has built up Trafalgar House over 30 years into a group embracing commercial and residential property, general contracting, civil, structural, offshore and specialist engineering, oil and gas exploration, shipping, aviation and hotels. Through organic growth and perhaps more through acquisition his group is capitalised at well over £1 billion. He understands acquisitions and the financing of them and there were two things which occurred in the spring and early summer of 1986 which he did not like and which, in retrospect, other people should have disliked too.

The first was the buying in by Guinness of 90 million shares or the 14.9 per cent stake in Distillers built up by Morgan Grenfell and other concert parties. This was going to have the effect of increasing the company's gearing to over 100 per cent and Sir Nigel could not see the point of it unless there was some other reason for doing it. (As we now know, there was—guarantees against losses on many or perhaps all of those shares.)

But Sir Nigel seemed alone in querying it. Even Lex in the *Financial Times* seemed enthusiastic, 'Presumably the post-acquisition gearing of Guinness was never the subject of any undertaking to the Office of Fair Trading. Otherwise there might have been some pained glances at yesterday's £270 million arrangement to buy in 90 million new Guinness shares for cancellation. Yet the advantages to Guinness shareholders are patent. The shares have been saved from the expected battering which they would have suffered if both Argyll and the supporters of Guinness had tried to get their holdings placed. Hit with only one barrel the shares actually closed higher than the 300p placing price. Further ahead the short-term increase in debt will weigh less heavily on Guinness's earnings than the additional shares that would have been in issue. If Guinness cannot squeeze £270 million of cash out of Distillers by about next Thursday week, it should not have been allowed to take the company over in the first place.'

Sir Nigel Broackes' worries about how the new company was going to be run were heightened further, first by his meeting with Saunders and Tom Ward on 7th May (this was the meeting when Ward asked him when he thought Ernest should become chairman) and secondly by the way Distillers board meetings were summoned at such short notice that he was never able to attend. In fact Sir Nigel had no further meetings with Ernest Saunders after 7th May even though he had been named in the takeover documents as a member of the new board. (Apparently no one had asked him if he wanted to be on the board. They just assumed he would want to.)

At the second of these hurriedly called Distillers board meetings one of the resolutions proposed in advance was to approve an increased interim dividend, to which Sir Nigel objected or at the very least wanted to query the necessity. He felt that one of his responsibilities as a non-executive director was to keep an eye on the finances as he could hardly be expected to contribute in discussions about the marketing of brands. If he was not going to be present he wanted to make sure that Risk was alerted. He therefore sent a long telex outlining his views and worries to Risk. He sent it to the Guinness head office and not to the Bank of Scotland. It was never passed to Risk but to Ernest Saunders instead.

Perhaps it was not surprising that Sir Nigel said rather wistfully in January 1987, 'Perhaps Charles Fraser and I should have got together'. Indeed they should, but they did not and the Guinness juggernaut rolled on. The famous, now notorious, circular to shareholders came out late on Friday, 22nd August, the beginning of the Bank holiday weekend.

### The Circular to Shareholders

Considering or perhaps because it had had to be submitted to the Bank of England, the Department of Trade, the Office of Fair Trading, the Takeover Panel, the Stock Exchange and the Scottish Office the circular was singularly bland and failed to give an answer to the question that had caused the extraordinary general meeting and the circular in the first place, namely, why was it necessary to promise to have a Scottish non-executive chairman when trying to win over shareholders in March and then drop him within a few weeks of the success of the takeover?

The circular actually said, 'Since April, certain members of the board have held discussions with Sir Thomas Risk, who in January had agreed to become non-executive chairman following the acquisition. These discussions covered various matters, including the manner in which it was felt that the company should be run. In the light of these discussions and the situation at Distillers, the board of Guinness concluded that it would not be in the best interests of the company and its stockholders for Sir Thomas to be elected chairman.'

We all now know that this was not the whole truth. Risk, Fraser, and Wood Mackenzie as well as the Guinness directors, Morgan Grenfell, Kleinwort Benson, Cazenove and Freshfields knew that. If the Bank of England, the Department of Trade, the Office of Fair Trading, the Takeover Panel, the Stock Exchange and the Scottish Office had questioned Risk or Fraser they would have had a rather different picture.

Indeed, Charles Fraser was surprised at hearing Sir Nicholas Goodison, chairman of the Stock Exchange, state on the radio that a full inquiry into the affair had been concluded and the Stock Exchange were content to let the shareholders decide at the forthcoming meeting. How could they have made a full inquiry into the whole affair when they had not questioned either him or, as far as he knew, Sir Thomas Risk? How could all these eminent authorities remain silent in the face of this document when they knew that it did not address the core of the matter correctly?

There were those that suspected that word came from 'on high'. Indeed, Alf Young wrote in the *Glasgow Herald* in January 1987 under the title, 'Number 10's role in stifling row over Guinness,' that 'The Prime Minister's office apparently intervened last summer in the Guinness affair to warn Scottish Secretary, Mr Malcolm Rifkind to tone down criticism of the then Guinness chief executive, Mr Ernest Saunders'.

This of course was fiercely denied, but there were those that believed that the instructions ran along these lines, Distillers was a badly run company as indeed was Guinness a few years ago. This man

Saunders may not be the sort that walks when he knows he's out but he is the man to win the game. Just as cricket has to accommodate Botham you accommodate Saunders.

Furthermore, as Raymond Johnstone, the chairman of the long-established Glasgow investment management company, pointed out in a letter to the *Financial Times*, 'It should be noted that the statement that the non-executive committee will not be disbanded except with the sanction of a special resolution of shareholders contained in the circular and endorsed by the Stock Exchange appears to be misleading. Since the articles of Guinness contain no such provisions and since shareholders are not being asked to alter them this structure has the same status as the original proposals. Should the Guinness board ever decide it was in the best interests of its company to abolish the committee without reference to shareholders there is no legal restriction to prevent it doing so by a simple board resolution—and indeed it would be the legal duty of the board so to do.'

Of less significance than the words about Risk or about the non-executive committee but equally misleading was the opening sentence of the circular, 'On Monday, 14th July 1986 your board announced my appointment as president of the company.'

Lord Iveagh was not appointed president and is still not president for as yet there is no power in the Articles of Association to so appoint him. Therefore to appoint him or indeed to give the non-executive committee real power the company's Articles of Association needed to be altered and that requires approval by 75 per cent of the shareholders. A majority was one thing but 75 per cent was quite another. Saunders was not that sure of his shareholders. Anyway this particular point was not very relevant. Who cared whether Lord Iveagh was president or not?

Plenty of people, however, cared whether statements made in formal takeover documents were true or not. How was everyone shaping up for the extraordinary general meeting scheduled for Thursday, 11th September? The two leading newspapers in Scotland, the *Scotsman* and the *Glasgow Herald*, bravely continued to criticise both the company and Ernest Saunders. The *Glasgow Herald's* business page headline on 26th August was 'Saunders wins day as City fathers hide behind blushes' and continued, 'Over the past few weeks, practically every organisation in the City with regulatory pretensions [a nice selection of words for "pretensions" was exactly what they were shown to be] has been drawn into the Guinness affair. Without exception they have been content to either pass the buck or rubber stamp proposals which fly off at a tangent to the main issue at stake.'

Alf Young, who had seen through Saunders from very early days, wrote in the *Scotsman*, 'Guinness smokescreen just obscures big questions'. Mr Young also had the courage to point out that Sir Norman Macfarlane, 'Mr Clean' as he was later dubbed by the *Sunday Telegraph*, was not only a compromised non-executive director in view of his position as a major supplier of bottle tops and labels to the Guinness group but also that his remark, 'There comes a time when everyone must stop crying foul and get on with the game' was a little premature. (In the light of subsequent events of course it was a pity everyone did not shout 'foul' a lot louder.)

Alf Young was also perceptive in pointing out that the so-called new power of the non-executive directors was an illusion. Two were already compromised, one as a major supplier and another as a major customer. They were matched by four executive Guinness members on the board and furthermore they were hardly likely to press the self-destruct button. In the event they were shown to be as toothless as Alf Young predicted. They made a great show of sacking Saunders on Wednesday, 14th January 1987 but this was only after the executive directors had demanded he resign the previous Friday.

In a way it was a pity that the Scottish newspapers were so virulent in their criticism—the leaders in the *Scotsman* lent their weight to Alf Young inveighing against 'the confidence trickster's art' and talking of the Stock Exchange's words being 'no less than a licence for the ruthless and dishonest'. But these harsh words, absolutely justified as they were, allowed the Guinness public relations machine to turn the conflict into a 'Scotland v England' match instead of a 'right v wrong' one.

John Chiene of Wood Mackenzie, himself a Scotsman, was only too well aware that the point of principle was being lost in this clever turning of the debate into a Scotland v England match. He spent many hours in meetings and on the telephone to institutions in London discussing the situation, but no major national institution would oppose the Guinness line and the Legal and General delivered a paean of praise to Saunders. (Some Apollo, whom even the gods feared. Certainly Chiene was beginning to feel that most of the City feared Saunders.)

David Barker, then an investment manager at the Norwich Union, now ironically working under John Chiene at Hill Samuel, was vociferous in his praise of Saunders and was roundly attacked by Alf Young in the *Scotsman*, 'David Barker, investment chief at the Norwich Union, sounds like the authentic voice of fund managers. What are a few broken promises or principles between friends, he seemed to imply last week, if the price is a 75p drop in the Guinness share price. Mr Barker was giving Ernest Saunders the benefit of the doubt describing the Scottish dimension in the Guinness crises as "peripheral" and generally paving the way for a judged solution to the Tom Risk affair.'

111

Alf Young then made a telling point, 'The trouble with fund managers like Mr Barker is that they themselves are judged on increasingly short-range performance criteria. How can they justify to their trustees or boards a principled decision to face Mr Saunders and the Guinness board out if it is going to cost them a £25 million slump in the value of their own holding of Guinness stock?' Mr Barker was not going to take this lying down and he wrote at length to the *Scotsman* on 4th August. Included in this letter was the comment, 'I reject the suggestion that short-term considerations colour my judgment. I hazarded a guess that the share price might drop by 75p if Mr Saunders is obliged to or decides to resign. That is some measure of his managerial reputation.'

This hypothesis has yet to be tested as Saunders has so far refused to resign as a director.

Mr Barker continued, 'But may I make it perfectly clear that Norwich Union would willingly pay that price if ultimately we decide that Mr Saunders' actions are unacceptable so that Guinness's long-term interests would best be served by a change of management'. Even in February 1987 Barker maintained that nothing had been proven against Saunders though he did admit that some of the circumstantial evidence was beginning to look a little daunting.

The English press, with the exception of the *Daily Mail* and the *Financial Times*, were duped. Kenneth Fleet wrote in *The Times* on 12th August, 'The structure is a good one. Indeed after the Bank of England and others pushed Guinness to appoint a strong non-executive committee, it looks a model for any company in which the roles of chairman and chief executive are combined. Nor can there be any argument that this is a far better board and management structure for the job than the pseudo federal arrangement put together when Guinness agreed terms with Distillers to fight off Jimmy Gulliver's Argyll Group.

Put simply, a mistake was made. It may have seemed convenient at the time, although the Scottish lobby and Distillers were long estranged. The directors are not threatening to resign over the issue, which is healthy. Shareholders, most of them former Distillers shareholders, must decide. They will have to choose between what is good for their pockets and what is good for high formal standards in public companies. But since the main point of those standards is itself to protect the interests of shareholders they may well think it illogical to oppose a board that however Mr Saunders may be cast in the Ian

21. Anthony Greener, managing director, Dunhill. One of the new non-executive directors.

22. Sir David Plaistow, chairman, Vickers. One of the new non-executive directors.

23. Ian Maclaurin,
chairman, Tesco. One of
the new non-executive
directors.

24. Ian Chapman,
chairman, William
Collins. One of the new
non-executive directors.

25. Tony Good, chairman, Good Relations. He helped Tom Risk stem the tide of abuse from the Guinness PR machine.

26. Sir John Nott, chairman, Lazards. Let down by his client GEC in 1985, he presumably felt let down by his client Guinness in 1986.

27. Sir Nicholas Goodison, chairman, the Stock Exchange. He did not feel it necessary to consult either Tom Risk or Charles Fraser before declaring Guinness' actions satisfactory in August 1986.

Directors   shareholding as at 26 September 1981

| Name | Personal Interests | Other Family Beneficial Interests | Other Interests |
|------|-------------------|----------------------------------|-----------------|
| Arthur Guinness Son & Co Ltd | Ordinary Stock (25p Units) | | |
| Earl of Iveagh | 1,666,916 | 3,923,000 | 4,170,996 |
| Hon. S.D.R. Lennox-Boyd | 506,286 | 1,335,480 | 699,692 |
| A.J.R. Purssell | 2,993 | – | – |
| A.P.B. Guinness | 27,000 | – | 10,000 |
| S.E. Darmon | 3,455 | – | – |
| M.B. Ogle | 273,670 | 384,558 | – |
| Viscountess Boyd | 182,970 | 82,976 | 3,230,516 |
| Hon. J.B. Guinness | 30,662 | 1,675,096 | 223,768 |
| C.E. Guinness | 9,701 | 8,368 | – |
| W.A.G. Spicer | 2,500 | – | – |
| M. Hely Hutchinson | 7,000 | 1,402 | – |
| M.R. Hatfield | 2,593 | – | – |
| Marquess of Dufferin and Ava | 22,220 | 2,401,390 | 2,718,030 |
| Hon. F.B. Guinness | 708,050 | 1,314,502 | 3,402,817 |

28.   The shareholdings of the Guinness family help to show why Saunders was so revered in 1986. Since his appointment the value had increased by seven times.

29. Ivan Boesky, the American king of arbitrageurs. When he lost his crown did he sing about Guinness?

30. Meshulam Riklis and Pia Zadora, American president of RCA and his wife. His subsidiary Schenley bought more than 5% of Guinness and 'forgot' to inform the Takeover Panel.

31. Paul Channon, Secretary of State, Trade and Industry. Embarrassed by the whole Guinness affair because of his family connection.

Botham role has in the end openly recognised its error.'

This was bad enough at the time. In the light of subsequent events it is ridiculous. 'The directors are not threatening to resign over the issue, which is healthy'—some thought it extremely unhealthy. 'The main point of those standards is itself to protect the interests of the shareholders'—the main point of high formal standards in public companies is to protect the interests of *all* shareholders in *all* companies, not the narrow interests of one set of shareholders in one company. Some might have concluded at the time that if Saunders was allowed to renege on one promise in 1986 that might or might not be in the interests of shareholders how long would it be before he performed some other misdemeanour that would definitely not be in the shareholders' interest. He had, of course, already performed it, and those same shareholders only had to wait three months to find out about it. (In his own mind Sir Nigel Broackes had given him three years before he tripped himself up.)

Finally Kenneth Fleet gave Saunders credit for 'openly recognising his error'. Far from doing this he resisted every sanction tooth and nail and seems to be a man who is completely incapable of recognising any error on his part whatsoever. When the Department of Trade inspectors walked in on 1st December he could not for the life of him think what they might be looking for. But if Kenneth Fleet confined himself to his views however erroneous, Ivan Fallon in *The Sunday Times* produced an article which is mind-boggling both for its inaccuracy and for its discarding of the basic principles on which the City has to function if it is to retain any credibility. In an article entitled, 'The hunt for Sir Tom', Fallon spends four long paragraphs explaining how the promise to make Sir Thomas Risk chairman of the new group does not appear in the offer document at all but only 'at the top of page eight of the listing particulars . . . it is all over in a paragraph'. On this basis Fallon concludes, 'Now it is clear to me that the central issue of this document was that shareholders in Distillers were being asked to decide between two people: Ernest Saunders of Guinness and James Gulliver of Argyll. Sir Thomas Risk, worthy gentleman as he undoubtedly is, does not come into it.'

In fact, Fallon was quite wrong. The details of the new board structure did not only appear on page eight of the listing particulars, they appeared on page six of a letter from Lord Iveagh and Ernest Saunders sent it to shareholders on 3rd March 1986 with the following words on the front, 'This document is important and requires your immediate attention'.

As for the comment that 'it is all over in one paragraph' how many paragraphs do you need to say who is going to be chairman and who the new directors are going to be?

Furthermore, the decision to appoint Risk was in the first press release announcing the merger and as everyone knew at the time was regarded as critical by both the Guinness and Argyll camps.

Fallon concluded this article by having a go at the Scots. 'It also exposes some constitutional issues: Malcolm Rifkind, the Secretary of State for Scotland, may well find he has stepped beyond his ministerial powers in surrendering to the Scottish lobby and giving Saunders a pompous wigging. Rifkind, and other government ministers, in their attempt to anticipate a Labour outcry, over-reacted. It has all played directly into the hands of those who demand the end of self-regulation, and the imposition of a clear and statutory SEC.'

Actually, of course, what has played into the hands of such people is the fact that Malcolm Rifkind and the rest of the authorities confined themselves to 'pompous wiggings' instead of insisting that promises must be kept. Some might also think that the whitewashing, even encouragement, of such behaviour by sections of the press that ought to know better also encouraged the 'we can walk on water' attitude of Saunders and his cronies and thereby also brought the days of statutory control that much nearer.

This attempt to play down the significance of the role of Tom Risk was in stark contrast to its significance in January. The Argyll camp were in no doubt that his proposed appointment as chairman was an absolute key factor in the battle. Strangely enough, Ian Macintosh on Saturday, 18th January 1986, the very day that Risk accepted Saunders' offer, had said, 'Guinness are going to bid and I expect they'll appoint someone like Tom Risk as chairman'. Also on that Saturday incidentally, as a result of the leak in *The Times* about Guinness getting involved, Gulliver had telephoned Saunders and asked him if there was anything in the rumours. Saunders had told him there was not.

Many sections of the so-called 'responsible' press, with the honourable exception of the *Financial Times*, were completely taken in by the weight of the Guinness public relations machine. It might be interesting here to note the attitude of Dewe Rogerson, one of Guinness' public relations consultancy firms, as expressed in February 1987. When questioned about their role, a spokesman,

Christopher Ashton Jones, said that since December 1986 it had been an arms length relationship and that he personally had not really been involved before September 1986. (Later he admitted that he had been present at a meeting until 2 a.m. with Saunders, Ward, Roux and Tim Bell on the night of Sunday 13th July, the night of the Ivan Fallon article about the ditching of Sir Thomas Risk.) When Mr Ashton Jones was asked who was responsible for looking after the Guinness account the answer was Roddy Dewe, chairman of Dewe Rogerson, who was on holiday until May and therefore uncontactable.

That then, would seem to be that, except that when it was suggested that Dewe Rogerson did not come out of the affair very well, a commercial director, Barry Kirkham appeared and spoke more openly of their role. Asked if Dewe Rogerson felt any obligation to check the veracity of any comments a client might ask them to make, Kirkham said that if he could be shown that Saunders or anyone else at Guinness had at any time misled them deliberately they would instantly resign. Prompted by this support Ashton-Jones claimed that Saunders likes to keep a close relationship with certain people in Fleet Street and would contact, even visit them, directly without using his public relations consultants.

Neither could see or would admit that Dewe Rogerson had done anything that might be criticised during last summer. They were perfectly happy about the way they organised the extraordinary general meeting (we shall see what others thought of it in a minute). Dewe Rogerson are still one of the public relations agencies employed by Guinness (there is another one as we shall see later). Some people might wonder quite what Saunders or anyone else at Guinness has to do before Dewe Rogerson feel that they have been deliberately misled.

The *Sunday Times'* concern for Guinness shareholders if Ernest Saunders' proposal that he be both chairman and chief executive was not allowed made sad reading. Ironically it was the *Sunday Times* 15 years earlier who had done so much to make Distillers face up properly to their responsibilities for selling Thalidomide. Quite rightly they had shown little concern for Distillers' shareholders on that occasion. Now they were saying that it was all right to go back on promises made in a takeover document because the alternative for shareholders was too horrendous to contemplate. What was horrendous about it, for goodness sake? If they were Distillers shareholders they had seen their holdings more than double between August 1985 and August 1986 and if they were Guinness shareholders they had seen their shares appreciate by six to seven times since 1981.

Incredibly, even after all the revelations of early 1987, Alex Murray of the *Sunday Telegraph* still believes that he made the right decision in recommending shareholdes to back Saunders, 'Money talks at the end of the day—and while I am sure the meeting will be lively and many will oppose these proposals, Saunders looks likely to win the day. He will, after all, be judged by shareholders on his performance as a manager—and his record, particularly as a marketing man, is good. I wish him well. But he and his new board will have to live with the (albeit short-term) credibility gap they have created.'

Melvyn Marckus in the *Observer* on the Sunday before the crucial vote of 11th September wrote, 'In a statement timed to cause maximum embarrassment to Guinness on Thursday, Risk alleged that the decision not to appoint him chairman was essentially presented as a *fait accompli*. Guinness's camp categorically deny this, and have consistently argued that the attendance of Risk at key management meetings immediately after the takeover of Distillers illustrates the company's initial intention to appoint Risk as chairman.'

As we already know Risk was not invited to attend any key meetings in the immediate aftermath of the takeover and indeed did not see Saunders until Sunday 18th May, when he was told that he was not required as chairman. Sir Nigel Broackes confirms that on 7th May Tom Ward said to him, 'When do you think Ernest can become chairman?'. John Bell of the *Sunday Express* questioned whether promises made in takeover documents were adhered to or not. Under the headline, Saunders looks good for Guinness, he wrote, 'The bigger issue now though, is not whether promises made in the pages of official takeover documents should be sacrosanct for all times, it is, as the circular to shareholders will explain, that those original promises were proving a disaster in practice. Not to face that fact would surely be folly or worse.'

Actually, what was folly was not to realise that a team that reneged on promises was also likely to be suspect.

## The Extraordinary General Meeting

As the day approached, the arguments raged. The Saunders camp supported by some of the press made great play of Risk using a public relations consultant. Here is Kenneth Fleet in *The Times*, under the headline, 'The risk no Guinness shareholder can take', he wrote, 'A clever finely orchestrated campaign by the Scottish commercial establishment will reach its crescendo in the Mount Royal Hotel, London tomorrow. The clans in Glasgow and Charlotte Square are baying for blood and the Scottish media bath daily in mass hysteria. The blood in particular they want is Ernest Saunders' who has been subject to malign and racist insults of a despicable kind. It is important for Guinness shareholders to recognise fully what the Scottish clique, in alliance with Kleinwort Benson, the closely related M and G and other southern supporters, are asking them to do when they vote tomorrow. They are being asked to undermine the position of Ernest Saunders and the Guinness board and senior management to the point where the group would become unmanageable.

No one may be irreplaceable but at risk here is an entire board. Therefore the [effect on the] Guinness share price if shareholders were to reject the first resolution would be painful. For that reason alone it would be inexcusable if any investing institution did not consider its obligation to those whose savings it holds and voted for the Guinness board. The voting ought, and I believe will, go in Guinness's favour. One of Guinness's difficulties in defending its corner is the contrast that has been skilfully drawn between the ambitious and abrasive Saunders and the dignified and constructive Risk, who has wanted "to keep away from personalities" but has been astute in the timing of his interventions—and even in his use of a professional public relations adviser.

Though Sir Thomas has seemed to keep a low profile leaving much of the campaign against Guinness to his close aides, Raymond Johnstone, chairman of Murray Johnstone, and Charles Fraser, the Scottish solicitor who left Morgan Grenfell with a great flourish on Monday, his role has been crucial notably in contesting the truth of Guinness statements about the course of his dealings with Guinness directors from the time the Distillers bid succeeded up to the final break in July. For the chairman of a major bank he has taken an extraordinary chance. Guinness insists that there are gaps in Sir Thomas's version which if revealed might shake some of the confidence placed in his account of events.'

So there we have it. Ivan Fallon in the *Sunday Times* thought the Secretary of State for Scotland was stepping out of line for telling Saunders off and now Kenneth Fleet was saying the same about Sir Thomas Risk, Governor of the Bank of Scotland for suggesting that Saunders was not telling the truth.

If Fleet had fully investigated Wood Mackenzie's resignation as the company's broker he would have discovered that they resigned with the full backing of Hill Samuel. To an outsider Risk was a man with an impeccable record, the 'very child of integrity', Saunders was a man of 'vaulting ambition'. As for the criticism of Risk's using a 'professional public relations adviser' it is scarcely believable. Guinness themselves not only used many in-house public relations officials (I was passed from one to another) but also several outside agencies. Peter Binns of Binns Cornwall, who you will remember, were appointed public relations consultants to Distillers, can remember attending meetings with Saunders during the bid battle when they were surrounded by public relations advisers, Dewe Rogerson, Biss Lancaster, Binns Cornwall and even Sir Gordon Reece. He can also remember that at one of those meetings in front of about 30 people Saunders was asked what the role of John Connell, then chairman of Distillers, the company with whom they were supposed to be having a friendly merger, would be. Saunders picked up a piece of paper and ostentatiously dropped it into the waste paper basket. Risk's public relations adviser was Good Relations. Good Relations had been handling the Bank of Scotland account for over a year and Tony Good, the managing director of Good Relations, had always acted personally on their account, and it was his colleagues at the Bank who urged Risk to seek assistance in countering the constant slurs coming from the Guinness camp.

As we shall see, Ivan Fallon was to take up this point about public relations consultants after the fateful extraordinary general meeting. But first the meeting—it took place on Thursday 11th September at the Mount Royal Hotel, London. The press took sides beforehand:

For Saunders—*Sunday Times, Observer, Sunday Telegraph, Sunday Express, The Times*

Against —*The Scotsman, Glasgow Herald, The Financial Times, The Guardian, Daily Mail*

The *Financial Times* produced a leader on the Monday entitled 'No-one is irreplaceable' and concluded, 'No-one is irreplaceable. In a statement last week, Sir Thomas Risk clearly implied that Guinness did not make serious efforts to fulfil its commitments. The company has yet to make a satisfactory explanation of what events which could not have been expected at the time of the offer subsequently led it to change its mind. The responsibility for controlling the behaviour of management does not lie with the Stock Exchange or with some statutory agency, but with shareholders. On the basis of its performance so far, Guinness does not deserve the benefit of the doubt. The posts of chairman and chief executive should be kept separate.'

Raymond Johnstone of Glasgow fund managers Murray Johnstone had written a weighty letter to the *Financial Times* the previous week deploring the Guinness behaviour and making the point that the much vaunted non-executive committee was in fact toothless. But very few were listening to voices from Scotland any more. They were assumed to be automatically pro-Risk and anti-Saunders.

## 'Pure Pantomime'

Sir Nigel Broackes, who has chaired and attended enough shareholders' meetings in his time described the extraordinary general meeting as 'pure pantomime' to Melvyn Marckus. To others he used a stronger word. It is of course normal at a shareholders meeting either to have microphones dotted around the audience or to have them moved to anyone who wants to speak. In this way a dialogue can be pursued between shareholders and the board. At this EGM shareholders had to queue to speak at one of two microphones placed either side of the rostrum. No sensible dialogue was possible.

The only serious contribution speaking against the resolution came from Graeme Knox of Scottish Amicable. He accused the Guinness board of 'cheating' Distillers and Argyll shareholders and attacked Saunders for his 'cynical and unwarranted' pay rise. (It had been revealed in the circular that Saunders' pay had been increased to £370,000 per annum.) It was somewhat unfortunate that Mr Knox with his red beard looked a little like a warring Scottish clansman. Again it looked like 'Scotland v England' instead of 'right v wrong.'

To the amusement of many and the delight of the Guinness board the next speaker was also a Scot but one who proceeded to attack the Scottish mafia opposing the righteous Saunders. A certain Mr Gillies congratulated Saunders for 'outsmarting and outwitting the Scottish mafia' led by 'godfather' Sir Michael Herries, chairman of the Royal Bank, with his 'bedfellows' Sir Thomas Risk and Charles Fraser. He rambled on until even the board requested him to stop. His intervention had, however, been effective.* No-one else seemed to want to criticise the board and there followed a series of speakers praising the board in general and Ernest Saunders in particular.

It was a great pity that the respected David Hopkinson, the chairman of M and G group, did not speak. He had made his views clear during August by declaring prophetically, 'The man broke his word. Such men should not be trusted in the City.'

Nobody challenged the remarks by Lord Iveagh that the Guinness board had not appreciated the full extent of Distillers' problems. This was arrant nonsense. On the day of their bid for Distillers in early December 1985, rival bidders Argyll had produced a comprehensive brochure showing exactly the extent of Distillers' problems, and circulated it widely.

'Do you realise,' said Iveagh, 'that Distillers' share of the UK Scotch whisky market has fallen from 54 per cent to 15 per cent?'. Gasps of amazement. What were they gasping about? It was all there last December in chart form on page three (not at the top of page eight of the listing particulars) of the brochure accompanying the press announcement of Argyll's bid.

Was this the sort of thing all of those who were supporting Saunders and those authorities who were 'leaving it to the shareholders' wanted from this company and its board? Unbelievably even a journal like the *Economist* fell for this line of patter too. On 4th October it wrote 'Guinness learnt only after the takeover of the severity of the many problems facing Distillers' Scotch whisky distilleries in the highlands of Scotland. The group would have to make much bigger cuts in whisky production than it had envisaged—a prospect that Sir Thomas apparently found difficult to live with.' Actually Risk was never asked. But it was good public relations for the Guinness cause. What is depressing is that the *Economist* fell for it.

Nothing of substance was said by Saunders about the reasons for

---

*No one there knew that Mr Gillies was not what he appeared to be—an ordinary Scottish shareholder. In fact, as Alf Young pointed out in the *Scotsman* the next day, Gillies had had a grudge against the Royal Bank of Scotland ever since they had foreclosed on his business, House of Hearing, three years before. He had lobbied the General Assembly of the Church of Scotland, had Sir Michael Herries dragged into court for contempt and sent Sir Michael a kiss-o-gram at the time of the merger with Williams and Glyn. The kiss-o-gram was a barrister with a joke summons.

dismissing Sir Thomas Risk and nothing further was said about setting up headquarters in Edinburgh. When he was asked when he was coming to live in Edinburgh, Saunders said his wife thought he lived at Heathrow. (The public relations boys had photographed her house-hunting in Edinburgh, Mrs Saunders told Gulliver she was looking in Oxfordshire and Saunders made a quip about Heathrow.) Finally the eulogies stopped and the proxy votes were revealed—322 million in favour, 27 million against. In view of what we know now, we can perhaps wonder how many of those proxy votes came from shares for which an indemnity had been given. A show of hands vote was also taken—also in favour. Graeme Knox wanted a proper poll but was brushed aside by Saunders. Again it was a shame that no one supported Knox so that the necessary two people could have forced a proper vote at the meeting. Sir Nigel Broackes left murmuring 'pure pantomime'. Tony Good was accosted by the Guinness in-house public relations official Chris Davidson who said to him, 'If I weren't such a gentleman I'd have had you thrown out'. John Chiene and his colleagues drove back to their office in absolute silence, so appalled were they, not at the result—they had expected that—but at the way the whole affair had been conducted.

## The Aftermath

Saunders was victorious. His enemies were routed. It was just left for Ivan Fallon to kick them while they were down, 'One point that emerges clearly from the Thomas Risk affair is that Guinness now has overwhelming support for *not* going to Scotland. In fact I'm not sure that it wouldn't have to seek shareholders' approval for a move of its main centre to Edinburgh after last week's overwhelming vote in favour of the board's resolution. The Scottish lobby made a lot of noise before Thursday's meeting but, when it came to the event itself, was struck mute with the exception of a balding Glaswegian called Graeme Knox of the Scottish Amicable who did not exactly rally the meeting behind him.

'The tone of the meeting clearly indicated that shareholders are not in the least interested in their company moving north of the border. The Scottish card was overplayed quite appallingly in the last two months. . . . This is to take nothing away from Saunders' victory. His fear was that he might win the vote but lose the propaganda war. Sir Thomas may have given him an early victory by suddenly emerging from behind the scenes to issue a statement through a well-known public relations company. Protests on points of principle somehow do not fit with public relations campaigns.' (Presumably they are satisfactory for revealing broken promises). 'All round the City—and maybe even in Scotland—one could almost hear the institutions turn down the decibels of their indignation'. Pro tem, Mr Fallon, pro tem. So everyone was left with a very sour taste in the mouth. Humour was not in abundance but Charles Fraser was to enjoy one hilarious incident in the Caledonian Hotel the day after the EGM.

He was having lunch with Rob Harman, the Unilever-trained new chief executive of Bell's. (This was slightly odd in view of Fraser's disaffection with the Guinness camp but the lunch had been arranged many weeks before when Saunders had asked Fraser to help Harman when he came to Scotland.) Fraser had offered, in the light of events, to cancel the appointment but Harman suggested they meet and confine the conversation to matters other than the Guinness affair.

While they were having lunch the former Scotland fly-half and current Anglo-American director, Gordon Waddell, clutching a collection of the day's papers all of which headlined the Guinness EGM, walked into the dining room. Recognising his friend, Fraser, he marched over to him and in a loud voice (the Waddells are not noted for the quality of their whispering) and without waiting to be introduced to Fraser's guest, immediately commented on the iniquity of this rascal Saunders and the Guinness affair and the damage that had been done to the City of London.

Fraser attempted to introduce Harman but the tirade against the disgrace of Guinness continued. Eventually Fraser explained to him who Harman was. Waddell, a most honest, open and enormously successful businessman, was undeterred.

The conversation then turned to more general matters and Fraser asked Waddell if he was staying in the Caledonian. That set Waddell off again, stating that it was not the hotel it used to be. Again Fraser attempted to explain that the Caledonian was also owned by Harman's company. Again undeterred Waddell told Harman of the inadequacies of the hotel.

So much for Fraser's attempts to have an uncontroversial lunch with Harman!

# SIX

## 'My genius is rebuked'

**'Double, double, toil and trouble
Fire burn, and cauldron bubble'**

'I've been scooped!' This was the cry of Peter Koenig, American journalist working then on the American monthly magazine, *Institutional Investor*, and now significantly, for *Euromoney*.

You will remember that the thing that first alerted Woodward and Bernstein to the Watergate scandal was seeing a senior White House official at the court hearing of a supposedly run-of-the-mill break-in at the Watergate complex. If it's so run-of-the-mill why is that guy here? they wondered.

Peter Koenig had a similar experience in November 1986, well before the Department of Trade and Industry moved into Guinness, and at a time when Saunders was still the hero of Fleet, Fallon, most fund managers and presumably, as his knighthood was on the way, the government.

Koenig had written an article in the April 1986 edition of *Institutional Investor* on mergers and acquisitions. It was called, 'British M and A's rather aggressive new look', and subtitled ominously 'Though London hasn't gone in for US-style takeover brawls—yet—the old gentleman's club rules are fast crumbling'. Peter Koenig is American and writes like an American using such phrases as, (and bear in mind this was in April 1986 not March 1987):

> 'thuggish way the battle has proceeded.'
> 'In the course of the five-months-long battle, Argyll and the Distillers–Guinness camp have each financed down-and-dirty public relations and advertising campaigns.'
> 'In the heat of the increasingly lucrative moment, takeover tactics once considered taboo in London have been introduced by City merchant bankers and, in particular, Morgan Grenfell, the city's leading—and most aggressive—takeover house. Non-establishment deal makers have taken their cues from the new rougher takeover methods adopted by Morgan Grenfell.'
> 'Meanwhile the authority of the Takeover Panel, which derives from nothing more than a City consensus, appears to be crumbling. "The Panel" says its executive director, Walker-Haworth, "acts as a kind of takeover referee for the City". The trouble is, fewer and fewer people are listening when the whistle blows.'

This was part of a larger article on mergers and acquisitions worldwide and Koenig was asked by his management to follow it up with an article on 'the deal of the year'. He decided that the Guinness takeover of Distillers was probably the deal of the year and during October and November set about interviewing the key people, including of course Saunders. His attempts to see Saunders all came to nothing and he had to settle for seeing the Guinness public relations officer, Chris Davidson.

In the meantime, Koenig had spoken to Rupert Faure-Walker, of merchant bankers Samuel Montagu, and asked why Guinness had won and was told that there were two reasons. The first was the appointment of Tom Risk and the second was the rise in the Guinness share price. Nothing very startling there. But Faure-Walker went on to elaborate about the rise in the Guinness share price and asked Koenig if he had noticed a recent press mention of Schenley securing distribution rights for Dewar's whisky and had he noticed Schenley's connection with Atlantic Nominees.

Koenig, during his interview with Davidson, mentioned Atlantic Nominees. The result was an invitation from Ernest Saunders, the man who had refused to see him, to come to a party at the National Gallery on 1st December to view the painting, which Guinness were lending to the Gallery. Immediately, Koenig knew he was on to something and wanted his journal, *Institutional Investor*, to run it. Unfortunately they showed little interest and within a few weeks of course the whole sorry tale was coming out anyway.

## 'Strange screams of death'

Between the extraordinary general meeting of 11th September 1986 and the walk-in of the Department of Trade and Industry (DTI) inspectors on 1st December 1986, it had been business as usual, whatever that might mean, at Guinness. This had been punctuated by

bursts of outrage at more broken promises, most notably by Alf Young in the *Scotsman*, he of the good memory and comprehensive notes. Young remembered that on 11th August 1985, one of the final days of the battle for Bell's, Saunders had flown to Glasgow and had said that if he won control of Bell's the Scottish hotels would not be for sale. 'I'm not doing deals with anyone on this issue.'

As Young pointed out, if anyone still needed reminding, such promises soon pale in the light of 'essential commercial reasons' (Lord Iveagh's favourite phrase) and the hotels were soon on the market and, although withdrawn during the battle for Distillers, were sold to the Norfolk Capital Group. Young was sufficiently perceptive or well-informed to note Morgan Grenfell's role in the affair and commented, 'The selling agent acting for Guinness is the property arm of Morgan Grenfell and the buyer, a hotel chain chaired by a director of that same merchant bank, no doubt cloaked for the occasion, in a Chinese dressing gown.' (Richmond-Watson had to show Saunders he could do something. Saunders had demanded that Seelig act for Guinness in the takeover of Distillers instead of Richmond-Watson.)

But in September, October and November 1986 no one was listening to Alf Young. They listened, open-mouthed, when it came across their television screens on Monday morning 1st December that DTI inspectors had marched into the company's headquarters at 9.30 a.m. and demanded access to the company's files. (Guinness expressed complete surprise, of course, but in fact they may have had warning because inspectors also went into the British Linen Bank in Edinburgh but not at 9.30 a.m., rather at 8.45 a.m. Ian Brown, the chief executive, said they were waiting for him when he arrived. 'He produced the papers giving him the necessary authority and asked to see all our files relating to the bid. He told me that he was as much interested in any annotations or scribbles in the margin as he was in the documents themselves.' This may have considerable relevance. The *Sunday Times* on 18th January 1987 opened an article on the Guinness scandal with the paragraph, 'The Department of Trade inspectors looking into Guinness are still spreading the net of their inquiry. Among the documents they would very much like to see are a set belonging to the sea-loving Washington lawyer Thomas Ward, who was last week "invited to resign" his directorship'. The documents were apparently unavailable.

The announcement of the raid immediately wiped 35p off the price of Guinness shares (less than half the 75p that Saunders' resignation would do according to Mr Barker) and helped send the *Financial Times* index down 19.7 points on the day. (It probably also wiped a few smiles off the faces of those marketing the flotation of British Gas as that Monday was the start of the final week of the flotation.)

## 'Acquaint you with the perfect spy o' the time'

The DTI inspectors were tight-lipped, but the Trade Department announced that it had brought into immediate effect provisions in the Financial Services Act 1986 which allowed its inspectors to disclose information to other regulatory bodies. The inspectors were to carry out their work under sections 432 and 442 of the Companies Act 1985. These sections provide for an investigation into suggestions that company officials have been guilty of 'fraud, misfeasance or other misconduct' towards the company or its shareholders, or when shareholders have not been given all the information they might reasonably expect. Under these sections the inspectors were able to investigate 'any circumstances suggesting the existence of an arrangement or understanding which, though not legally binding, was likely to be relevant to the investigation'.

The inspectors might have been tight-lipped but the City and the press had no doubts—Ivan Boesky, the recently disgraced American *arbitrageur*, had spilt the beans. Andrew Alexander in the *Daily Mail* pulled no punches in his article the next day, 'Boesky had been operating in that massive battle (Guinness/Distillers/Argyll). His purchase of Distillers' shares before Guinness made its first move had been variously estimated at the time. One suggestion yesterday was that he had bought as much as £100 million of Distillers shares in early January, the Guinness bid having been made in late January. Another recollection was that as the battle moved towards its climax, Boesky was said to have gone short of Argyll shares in a big way. That depressed the Argyll price and reduced the value of that company's offer for Distillers.'

This Boesky connection was to assume a much greater significance a few days later. For the moment everyone assumed he had been 'singing like a bird' which along with US $100 million had been the price of his freedom from penalties for insider dealing.

## 'Masking the business from the common eye'

The newly formed *Independent* newspaper, which was to secure some notable firsts over the coming weeks, immediately pointed out the Schenley/Atlantic Nominees connection, 'Knowledge of the connection between Atlantic and Schenley was not admitted until the shareholders' meeting at which Atlantic used its 4.5 per cent stake [remember that 4.5 per cent] in Guinness to support Mr Saunders' controversial campaign to reform the structure of the Guinness board. Schenley, which is owned by Meshulam Riklis's Rapid American Corporation, one of the largest privately owned companies in the United States, has since had its concession to distribute Dewars extended.'

So after the first day the speculation was that the investigation must be something to do with the takeover of Distillers, that Boesky was the tip-off man and that Schenley was involved. The second day brought confirmation, not speculation, that the inspectors were indeed focusing on the movement of the Guinness share price during the bid for Distillers. Confirmation came from George Law, the compliance officer at Guinness's merchant bank adviser, Morgan Grenfell. It also came from Guinness's two stockbrokers at the time of the bid, Wood Mackenzie and Cazenove. All three, Morgan Grenfell, Wood Mackenzie and Cazenove had been visited by representatives of the DTI inspectors.

Meanwhile the Guinness share price continued to fall—to 285p— that was 45p so far. Argyll were prompted to remark that they had been concerned about share price movements during the bid (they constantly but unavailingly complained to the Takeover Panel at the time), 'In the three weeks before the bid, every afternoon when Wall Street opened, the Guinness price would go up and ours would go down. Our shares were being shorted consistently and theirs were being propped up.'

In these early days of the DTI inspection Kenneth Fleet had a change of heart. Maybe it was not such a good idea after all to combine the roles of chairman and chief executive, 'If the investigation cannot be carried out properly except over months, it would raise a very difficult question for the Guinness board and in particular for Mr Ernest Saunders. Would it make sense, during a lengthy investigation for him to attempt three jobs: responding to the inquisitors, presiding as chairman and overseeing and directing the group as chief executive.' No Mr Fleet, it was never a good idea and it was not getting any better.

## 'Scotland hath foisons'

Amidst all the rumour and speculation Guinness showed it had not completely lost its powers to stage a public relations coup. On Wednesday, 3rd December 1986 it announced the appointment of the fifth non-executive director promised as long ago as August. Furthermore he had strong Scottish connections though, as the *Independent* pointed out unkindly, he lived in Cheam in Surrey. He was Mr Ian Chapman, the chairman and chief executive of William Collins, the Glasgow publishers. What he said publicly was that he was offered the job in October but that the appointment had to be ratified by the board at their bi-monthly meeting yesterday (the Guinness board was suddenly becoming very powerful). What he said privately was that he had had his arm severely twisted by the Scottish Office. He had in fact supported Argyll in the takeover battle the previous winter.

The announcement of Ian Chapman's appointment was the only positive thing to happen to Guinness in that first week. On the Thursday, Andrew Alexander, like Alf Young, a long-time critic of Guinness and its ways of going about its business, drew attention to the deal done with Lonrho at the time of the Distillers bid, 'The matter which needs investigation is that purchase by Tiny Rowland's Lonrho of the 10 whisky brands which Guinness' Ernest Saunders sold to reduce the Distillers share of the domestic Scotch market from 35 per cent to 25 per cent—thus avoiding a Monopolies and Mergers reference. The price paid was the oddity: £10.5 million—of which £7 million was for stock. This suggested that the domestic Scotch market was worth a mere £35 million.'

What Alexander did not say but might have done is that if the whole market is only worth £35 million why did Guinness pay £390 million for Bell's who had 21 per cent of that market?

## 'False face must hide what the false heart doth know'

If Fallon and Fleet did not like Sir Thomas Risk making statements through Tony Good we must wonder what they made of the battery of public relations agencies and operators Saunders now assembled to protect himself. (Come to that we must wonder what Saunders himself thought of it as they proceeded to trip each other up and make statements which were disproved by the next day's fresh set of revelations.)

The Sunday papers of 7th December were of course full of the story. The *Sunday Telegraph* had made contact with the Morgan Grenfell whizz-kid Roger Seelig. He said, 'Nor are we at Morgan Grenfell aware of any special arrangements, contacts or other relationships between Guinness and Boesky, or between Guinness and Schenley'. The *Observer* went a little further and elicited from Seelig that he knew Boesky, 'Of course I knew him. He knows me. That is his job.'

*The Observer* also highlighted Saunders' connections with Sir Gordon Reece (was he the 'good contact' that Saunders had boasted of when Fraser had warned him about a reference to the Monopolies and Mergers Commission?) and said that Saunders had contacted him immediately after the DTI inspectors walked in. Finally the *Observer* understood that Guinness was now 'employing the services of Andrew Gifford, a partner of GJW Government Relations, specialists in the art of political lobbying.' And of course as the *Scotsman* pointed out under its headline, 'Guinness calls in battery of legal and PR advisers', there was also Dewe Rogerson, Freshfields and Lazards, and though no one mentioned it there was Hill and Knowlton, appointed because Dewe Rogerson would not do what Saunders wanted them to do. They wanted Saunders to make no comment. According to them he wanted to hit back publicly and appointed Hill and Knowlton. David Wynne Morgan, the manager director of Hill and Knowlton, sees it differently. He says that he was already being asked to make a presentation as to how his company would handle the Guinness account on a worldwide basis, particularly in the USA and Japan (Hill and Knowlton are the biggest financial public relations consultancy in the world). Wynne Morgan is proud of the fact that he is a forthright PR man and feels that presumably, Saunders thought he was the right man for this crisis.

When asked if he had any worries about becoming involved in such a situation, Wynne Morgan said he had asked Saunders whether there had been any misdemeanours. Saunders replied that there clearly had been but he knew nothing of them. On that assurance Wynne Morgan took on the job.

In the second week of the inquiry all these advisers had something good and positive to say about the company when it published its first substantial trading report since the Distillers takeover. *The Times* even went so far as to shout, 'Gloom clears at Guinness', and Kenneth Fleet, faithful to Saunders to the end, said, 'In particular the Scottish lobby is baying for Saunders' blood. Whether they succeed in getting it will turn on the DTI's findings but rarely can any man, least of all the head of a leading company, have been so vilified as Ernest Saunders is in an early day motion put down in the Commons on 20th November.'

## 'Disguising what they are'

But the coterie of advisers did not have long to rejoice. On Friday 12th December 1986 it was revealed that Schenley had failed to disclose a holding the previous April of more than 5 per cent of Guinness shares (no wonder Koenig's mention of Atlantic Nominees had brought an invitation to the National Gallery). In its statement Schenley went on to say that its interest after the bid was reduced and that it now held 3.5 per cent. This gave the impression, as was presumably intended, that shares had been sold. In fact what it meant was that if it had 3.5 per cent of the enlarged group it must have bought 11.4 million shares in Distillers as well as the 17.6 million Guinness shares it confessed to.

This of course was all too much for the Sunday newspapers especially as the boss of Schenley, the controversial and unpronounceable Meshulam Riklis was married to the glamorous and equally unpronounceable Pia Zadora. Guinness's shareholders were then treated to revelations of Saunders', 'friends across the water'. Some of them at least must have been wondering why they had not voted for the less glamorous but more stable Sir Thomas Risk to look after their investment.

The *Sunday Times* (the story this time was entrusted to Peter Wilsher not Ivan Fallon) revealed, quite correctly, that Riklis had approached Gulliver when he had first bid for Distillers and offered to support him. It also said, again correctly, that in return Riklis wanted a guarantee of the continuing distributorship of Dewar's whisky. Gulliver said he was giving no guarantees but if he won the battle all marketing arrangements would be reviewed. Riklis was clearly not very happy and began to buy Distillers and Guinness shares through his then anonymous vehicle, Atlantic Nominees. Ultimately, Schenley not only retained the Dewars distributorship but also acquired the valuable Gordon's gin franchise as well.

## 'This sore night hath trifled former knowings'

Hardly had everyone had time to digest Meshulam and Pia when the

*Independent*, first again, revealed on Thursday 18th December 1986, that Guinness had invested US $100 million, yes $100 million, in a Boesky company. Only the week before Saunders had said 'I do not know these people.' What were the reactions to this piece of news?

The market marked the shares down 19p to 280p (now 50p below the price on 1st December). The public relations company, Hill and Knowlton in the shape of David Wynne Morgan said, 'It was like putting money in the bank'. The Guinness non-executive directors scrambled for separate legal advice and from the media came howls of agony and derision— 'They (the institutions who backed Guinness in the Risk affair) have had the wool pulled over their eyes, and they do not like it . . . Guinness suffered no lapse of concentration in not disclosing the investment . . . thought about it but decided against when the DTI called . . . The non-executive directors, bless 'em, went along with the silence.' Andrew Alexander, of course, leapt on the revelation with glee, 'The Guinness controversy .·. . seems to go on and on.' (Actually, there was plenty more to come.) . . . 'One problem about the link is obvious. The agreement to back Mr Boesky was reached in May, shortly after Guinness won the Distillers takeover battle, supported by Mr Boesky. Since a decision on an investment of that order and of that nature is unlikely to have been reached quickly the implication is that it must have been under consideration while the bid was on and while Mr Boesky's support was being canvassed.'

Alexander went on to point out the obvious question—How did they expect to keep it secret? Where was the logic? (After all had they not criticised Distillers for investments in oil and banking?) What did the rest of the Guinness board think about it? Others asked, had the company broken Stock Exchange rules on disclosures to shareholders? How could Saunders and Boesky not have met? And if they had not was it normal practice for Guinness to place US $100 million in the hands of a man that the chairman and chief executive had not met?

David Wynne Morgan was undaunted by his comment that an investment in Boesky was 'like money in the bank'. Questioned about it, he replied that he had attended a meeting with Saunders and Marcus Agius of Lazards and that this had been the agreed official line. Even if Saunders thought it a sensible thing to say surely Agius must have realised that it would be torn to pieces. Indeed it was by other investors in Boesky. Other investors included Gerald Ronson's Heron Group, the Water Authorities' superannuation fund, Commercial Union and J. Henry Schroder Wagg. A senior executive from one of them said, 'I don't think that as a limited partner one had any right to withdraw funds. I don't believe a fund of that nature could be organised on any other basis.'

How could money be taken in and out like at a bank? It was a long-term, at least five years, commitment. More seriously, in view of Boesky's fall from grace, it was by no means certain that Guinness would get its money back at all.

But Wynne Morgan was being paid to make comments (Dewe Rogerson had advised Saunders to make no comments) and his next gem as everyone began to talk of Saunders' resignation was to describe such suggestions as 'nonsense' and that Mr Saunders was 'extremely angry' about them. Wynne Morgan was not alone however. Marcus Agius of Lazards, now brought in to replace Morgan Grenfell, called the suggestions 'extraordinary' and 'quite bizarre' and Tesco chairman, Ian Maclaurin, one of the Guinness non-executive directors said that 'about the last thing he would do' would be to call for Mr Saunders' resignation.

### 'Whither should I fly? I have done no harm'

Christmas was coming. You could tell. In the middle of an article in the *Sunday Telegraph* entitled 'Split danger at Guinness—Saunders denies "quit" rumour', there were some sprigs of holly and mistletoe. Was someone now doing to Saunders what he had done so skilfully—planting leaks? The Lex column in the *Financial Times* was focusing on Saunders, 'Guinness's misfortunes have the concentrated power that comes of easy identification with one man—Ernest Saunders. That is now coming to haunt the majority of institutions which rallied to Mr Saunders' support in September over his abandonment of the joint Distillers/Guinness board structure. Their fear was that the value of their investment would fall sharply if Mr Saunders resigned . . . But now the Guinness shares have suffered such damage as to remove even the most tenuous management premium. . . The defence of the $100 million investment in the Boesky fund mounted so far by Guinness is unimpressive. . . . For Guinness to say that its investment amounted to "only" 4 per cent of assets is weird. It is even odder, set against the pledge of the new management to do everything in its power to reduce the very high level of post-merger gearing.'

The *Observer* was also asking two questions: 'If there are more potential skeletons should he (Saunders) release them? Has his own value to Guinness now become over-priced?' and concluded, 'Ernest Saunders must be asking himself whether he is still good for Guinness.'

If the newspapers were posing the question, some of the fund managers and analysts were in no doubt. Said one, 'For Guinness to have invested £70 million in an arbitrage fund without the chief executive having met the person responsible for the fund is simply preposterous.' Alan Gray, drinks analyst at brokers Campbell Neill said, 'There could be more disclosures yet. Mr Saunders has lost his credibility and, taking everything into account, I think he should resign'. Prescient, Mr Gray.

In spite of all we have seen and heard so far Kenneth Fleet was unrepentant. His 'hero' Saunders was the victim of a dastardly Scottish plot. This is what he wrote in *The Times* on Christmas Eve, 'It would be equally erroneous not to recognise that since the Risk-affair a powerful campaign has been mounted to punish Ernest Saunders and if possible to have him evicted from Guinness. This campaign originated with the Scottish establishment which turned on Mr Saunders, ostensibly for his broken undertakings to shareholders but in reality because they realised that control of "a great Scottish company"—the rundown Distillers which had gone to Ernest Saunders as a white knight who would save them from the dreaded Jimmy Gulliver—was about to be taken from Scotland.'

Andrew Alexander's Christmas message to his readers in the *Daily Mail* was to point out that the supposedly all-powerful, non-executive directors did not have the power to remove the chairman without a change in the Articles of Association. (Raymond Johnstone had said just that in his letter to the *Financial Times* just before the extraordinary general meeting in September.) This was not one of Alexander's best articles. He also complained that a fifth non-executive director, though promised, had not yet been appointed. As we have seen, Ian Chapman was appointed in early December.

Just before the break for Christmas a little light relief emerged when the *London Evening Standard* revealed that the 'Guinnessty' family affair included more than the Department of Trade Minister, Paul Channon. It pointed out that the first wife of David Wynne Morgan (he of the 'money in the bank') was married to none other than Michael Howard, the man who had sent in the DTI inspectors.

# SEVEN

# 'Now God help thee, poor monkey'

**'And each new day a gash is added'**

If December had brought excitement and revelation—the DTI, Schenley, Boesky—January 1987 was not to disappoint. Indeed before December was over it was revealed that a cheque for £48,000 was flying about in the City with no one to anxious to grab it and cash it. The cheque was the dividend on a block of 2.15 million Guinness shares which merchant bank Henry Ansbacher had acquired on behalf of clients at the height of the bid battle. Apparently Morgan Grenfell had asked Ansbacher to help in buying Guinness shares. The Ansbacher chief executive, Richard Fenhalls, had refused. Lord Spens, the Ansbacher chairman and former boss of Seelig at Morgan Grenfell was keen on the idea and, without telling Fenhalls, suggested to some Ansbacher clients that they buy them.

According to Spens, the clients wanted to sell the shares once the bid was over and he was approached by Morgan Grenfell who said they would buy them. Apparently Morgan Grenfell wanted to dispose of other shares and did not want to see the price fall. Morgan Grenfell then paid £7.6 million or 355p a share, to Down Nominees, a subsidiary of Ansbacher. This was well above the Guinness price on 18th April 1986 which opened at 335p and closed at 315p.

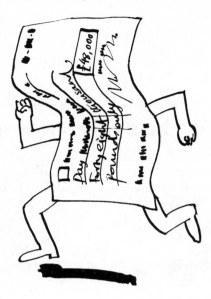

These activities had first been revealed in the Sunday newspaper on 28th December 1986. By Tuesday, 30th December, the *Financial Times* was talking of Ernest Saunders facing 'A fine or prison sentence, if he were implicated in any illegal purchases of Guinness shares or in giving assistance to other purchasers of the shares'.

Lex, as usual, was hitting hard, 'If the affair was not so upsetting it would be almost comical. The idea that Ansbacher, which had formed a relationship of mutual detestation with Guinness during the battle for Arthur Bell, should have been involved in covert support for Guinness against Argyll is bizarre, particularly if it is true. There is also the guest appearance of the genuine bouncing Guinness dividend cheque which nobody wants on the premises when inspectors from the DTI call. The more the DTI/Guinness story unravels, the more it seems to revolve around the possibility of undisclosed concert parties—on both sides of the Atlantic. And as a result of yesterday's allegations the City will more than ever want to know the reason behind the purchase of millions of Guinness shares by the Distillers pension fund just after Guinness took control of Distillers.'

By the first day of the new year the argument about who had bought the shares was now involving Guinness itself. Ansbacher said it was Guinness, Morgan Grenfell said it was Guinness, Guinness said it was

Morgan Grenfell. Sir David Napley, the well-known criminal defence lawyer, and by now appointed by Saunders to act for Guinness said, 'If they want to give their version of events they will tell it to the inspectors and we will give ours'. Whose nerve would crack first?

## 'There's daggers in men's smiles'

On 30th December 1986 the first head rolled. Roger Seelig, whizz-kid takeover specialist, was fired by Morgan Grenfell who, in turn, also resigned as advisers to Guinness. Peter Koenig, the 'perceptive' American journalist, had warned Seelig he was being set up as a sacrificial lamb. He had spoken to him on his car telephone:

'Who by?'
'The government.'

'The government!? Who in the government?'
'Gordon Reece.'

'Gordon would never do that to me.'
'I would like to come and see you, if I may, Mr Seelig.'

Koenig went to see Seelig at Morgan Grenfell the next day. This was an achievement in itself for by this time all such people were hiding behind their lawyers. Seelig agreed to see Koenig with the Morgan

Grenfell public relations man, the aptly named Byron Ouzey, but when Koenig arrived Seelig saw him alone at first, 'Is there anything you would like to tell me before I call in Byron Ouzey?' To which Koenig replied, 'No'.

Ouzey was then called and Koenig asked both of them routine questions about his assignment, 'The deal of the year'. Finally he said to Seelig 'Ward's the bad guy in all this, isn't he?' Seelig's response was—a smile. Koenig warned Seelig again, 'Mr Seelig, your colleagues are going to throw you to the wolves.' Seelig replied, 'Now you're making me very angry. We're very solid here.'

There's daggers in men's smiles.

## 'I have lost my hopes'

By the weekend of 4th January 1987 the press were openly speculating on the day of Saunders' resignation. The *Mail on Sunday* under the ingenious title, 'Is Genius in danger of losing its head?', wrote, 'Ernest Saunders is likely to resign as chairman of Guinness within the week'.

Alex Murrey in the *Sunday Telegraph* posed a list of 10 questions he felt Saunders should answer without delay on his return from his ski-ing holiday. (If he had hoped things might quieten down while he was away, they had not.) The questions of course ranged across the Ansbacher deal, Boesky, Schenley, share rigging, Bain and Co. and Sir Thomas Risk. But the most startling revelation of all was that in the *Observer* under the title, 'Director paid for shares in Guinness.' They had discovered that the famous Ansbacher shares had been bought with a transfer the authorisation for which has been signed by the finance director and Bain employee, Olivier Roux.

The row now became furious and open. *The Times* published details of correspondence between Richard Fenhalls and Ernest Saunders. Saunders was claiming that £7.6 million was an interest free deposit. Ansbacher claimed that the £7.6 million was used to buy the 2.15 million Guinness shares. The sum of £7,614,862 and 10p exactly covered the cost of buying the shares, the stamp duty and the financing of the position during the time the institutions held them.

In the meantime, the bunker mentality grew; the DTI were coming from the west and the press were arriving in hordes from the east and the company was lashing out in all directions. The *Financial Times* on Monday 5th January said, 'Guinness may act against press'. On Tuesday *The Times* announced 'Guinness may sue Ansbacher'. Whose turn was it to be on Wednesday—Morgan Grenfell? No, it was Ansbacher again.

On Tuesday, Sir David Napley, now acting for Guinness, sent a letter to Ansbacher demanding the return of the £7.6 million by 20th January. 'If the money is not repaid we will issue a writ.'

## 'Where are these gentlemen?'

With the executive of Guinness paralysed, what were the non-executives, supposedly appointed as a check on the executive, doing? The answer seemed to be—plenty of talking but not much doing. A board meeting, called at short notice (some things at least had not changed) resolved nothing except that Saunders was staying on as chairman and chief executive. However, a full board meeting was promised for the following Wednesday, 14th January 1987.

## 'Our fears in Banquo Stick deep'

Just as Morgan Grenfell had sacrificed Seelig, Guinness were clearly preparing to cut off Olivier Roux. On Wednesday 7th January in a statement denying any wrongdoing Guinness singled Roux out as the executive most familiar with the affairs under investigation. The signs were there for all to read and the *Independent* read them correctly. On Friday 9th January under the heading 'The exit beckons at Guinness', it predicted that Roux would be gone within the week and that Saunders would either step aside as chairman, at least for the duration of the DTI investigation, or would be forced to leave the company altogether.

In the event the *Independent* was not quite right. Saunders stepped aside *and* he was forced to leave the company altogether. To keep conversation going in the bunker other investors in the Boesky fund were now suggesting that Guinness would probably lose US $20 million of the US $100 million investment. Commercial Union were saying that the assets of the fund had declined by 20 to 25 per cent. Commercial Union also gave a warning, 'The very biggest of all unknowns is what the third party claims against the partners will be'.

## 'Poor prattler, how thou talk'st!'

If Seelig was bounced out of Morgan Grenfell with only the time to mutter dire threats, the Bain-trained Roux was going to do better than that. Ironically in November, just before the Guinness scandal broke, the magazine *Business* produced a long article on the country's top 40 businessmen under 40 years of age. Two of them were Olivier Roux and Anthony Salz of Freshfields. They were together in the text and on the same page of full-length portrait photographs. In the story on Roux the article said, 'For the time being, he is keen to stay with Guinness—but several other options are open to him, among them that of starting his own business. Roux is not particularly concerned about which sector this might fall in, but more about the intrinsic worth of any such enterprise.'

Roux, advised by his own lawyer as soon as the DTI investigation began, had seen the inspectors with his lawyer and had composed a letter. This letter was also sent to Sir David Napley. From there it was circulated to the Guinness directors. It revealed details of a massive £200 million campaign to support the Guinness share price during the Distillers bid (what a lot of fuss there had been over a mere £7.6 million) and it implicated Saunders completely, 'I do not agree that I was the financial man in charge of Guinness. I was a consultant seconded to Ernest Saunders. At all times many decisions I made were on behalf of Ernest Saunders.'

Roux also explained how he had been prevented by the American lawyer, Tom Ward, from co-operating with the company's solicitors, Freshfields. Saunders denied all the allegations but his executive directors were badly shaken. Brian Baldock, Vic Steel and Shaun Dowling were all appointees of Saunders, as indeed, of course, was Roux. But Roux, though only 36, is a cool customer, and his allegations (which also implicated himself) appeared unfortunately, only too accurate.

## 'Thou liest, thou shag-ear'd villain!'

Baldock, Steel and Dowling finally confronted Saunders on the evening of Friday, 9th January. That day, the second edition of the *London Evening Standard* had shouted in two-inch headlines on its front page, 'Saunders must step down', attributing the comment to board director Jonathan Guinness (the leaking technique had been well and truly learnt by this time). The newspaper also suggested that other board members, including Lord Iveagh (no doubt for 'pressing commercial reasons') agreed.

This brought an anguished outcry from the bunker and in the late edition the story had been relegated to page two and under the half inch headline, 'Row over *Standard's* Guinness story, the *London Evening Standard* said that Jonathan Guinness was now protesting that he had been misinterpreted. The redoubtable David Wynne Morgan stepped in again with this statement, 'Following a report in to-day's *Evening Standard*, Jonathan Guinness said: "I have never advocated that Ernest Saunders should step down as chairman. I did say that he is a man under intense pressure and that the pressure must be relieved".' (Is that not 'Kremlinesque' for saying that he must stand down as chairman?) ' "I specifically told the reporter that I had not had any communication with any member of the family since the DTI inquiry was announced and had no knowledge of any change in their views." '

Jonathan Guinness was going to appear on television Channel 4 that evening to deny that he wanted Saunders to stand down but during the afternoon he was visited by Steel and Baldock. They showed him the Roux letter. It was enough. The television appearance was cancelled. In the bunker, the three generals asked for a meeting with their leader. He was told it was about a routine communications matter. In fact the three were demanding that Saunders step down. According to the *Financial Times* one of the three said, 'It was an unfortunate, unhappy, emotional meeting'. After an initial meeting where the directors asked Saunders to step aside, he asked for time to think about it. He then retired to the Churchill Hotel where his wife and daughter were waiting for him. After a time they all returned to Guinness' offices and had to wait in the bar downstairs until the directors were ready to talk to him. It was a sad end.

So at last it had happened. It had seemed inevitable to most since the revelation of the Boesky involvement before Christmas. To some it had seemed inevitable at some stage since the events of the previous summer. (The Guinness share price instead of falling 75p actually rose 7p to 303p just 27p below the 330p of 1st December.)

In view of their role, Baldock, Steel and Dowling must have had mixed feelings about finding themselves placed in the 'for Saunders' camp the next morning in *The Times* Business News. In view of his role, Roux must have been utterly amazed to find himself in that group too. The Guinness family representatives were probably content seeing themselves sitting on the fence in the middle, and the non-executives were probably quite happy to see themselves placed firmly 'against'. Their moment of action was about to come. *The Times* certainly got one person in the right spot. Proudly on top of the 'for' camp was Tom Ward, grinning broadly.

He was not likely to be grinning for long. Attention now turned from Saunders to others. Who would be the next to fall?

Roux—only a matter of time, surely.
Ward—people were beginning to realise his key role.
Furer—people were about to be stunned by his role.
Reeves—did he really not know what Seelig was doing?
Walsh—the same as Reeves.
Mayhew—member of the war cabinet; how much did he know?
Salz—the same as Mayhew.
Lord Spens—is it normal practice to do something your chief executive expressly forbids and still survive?

### 'We have scotched the snake, not kill'd it'

Lex in the *Financial Times* on the Monday after this dramatic weekend expressed some sympathy with the non-executive directors with a delicious turn of phrase, 'To be an independent director of Guinness must be one of the least enviable honours that the business world has to offer. After being appointed in the rather optimistic hope of putting an occasional stopper on the Saunders fizz, the five independents are now engaged in the task of mopping up after the bottle has exploded.' The weekend had seen the appointment of one of the independents, Sir Norman Macfarlane, as chairman and Monday brought the next, inevitable casualty—Olivier Roux. The board meeting on Wednesday, 14th January, conducted in a half-deserted London as snow paralysed British Rail, unceremoniously sacked Ernest Saunders as chairman and chief executive and asked for his resignation as a director. It was also resolved to send letters to Ward and Furer requesting their resignation as directors.

### 'In the cauldron boil and bake
### Eye of newt and toe of frog'

On the morning of this board meeting, the *Independent*, first yet again, revealed details of a worldwide network of secret share dealings stretching from London to Zurich and New York to Vienna. Bank

Leu, one of Switzerland's oldest banks, (the chairman of which was Artur Furer, also a director of Guinness) was said to be involved in deals involving Guinness shares worth £100 million. By Friday, Sir Norman Macfarlane was able to make this statement on Bank Leu in a letter to shareholders, 'In the last two weeks, a number of serious disclosures have been made to the board and I feel it is important that I inform you forthwith of their main substance. It has been alleged that during and after the bid for Distillers, substantial funds of the company were applied in a widespread series of transactions involving both the purchase of its own shares and the giving of financial assistance with a view to their purchase. In particular, it has been established that substantial purchases of both Guinness and Distillers shares were made by wholly-owned subsidiaries of Bank Leu AG on the strength of Guinness' agreement, signed on its behalf by Mr Ward or Mr Roux, to repurchase the shares at cost plus carrying charges—an agreement which, at least as regards its own shares, Guinness could not lawfully have fulfilled. It is also alleged that these purchases may have been financed by lines of credit granted by Bank Leu AG. In connection with these purchases, and in apparent breach of Companies Act requirements, a Guinness subsidiary made a deposit of £50 million with a Luxembourg subsidiary of Bank Leu AG. The present position is that the £50 million deposit remains and a total of approximately 41 million Guinness shares are held by the Bank Leu Group.'

The bank themselves held a press conference in Zurich and issued its own version of affairs, 'In April 1986 the first business relations between Guinness and Bank Leu took place. On behalf of Guinness two Swiss companies of our group acquired both Guinness and Distillers stock. This purchase was financed by Bank Leu. It was specified that Guinness would re-acquire these positions at cost plus customary commissions and charges levied by the two group companies. In May 1986 one of the two acquired a further block of Guinness shares. This transaction was financed by Bank Leu (Luxembourg) SA. Once again this was a buy-back agreement with Guinness.

In terms of further security to cover the claims of Bank Leu under the three repurchase agreements a Guinness subsidiary pledged a £50 million time deposit maintained with Bank Leu (Luxembourg) SA in favour of the Bank Leu group. Thus Bank Leu currently holds close to five per cent of Guinness' outstanding common stock—that is around

41 million shares, representing an aggregate value of about £115 million. The build-up of Guinness' stock position out of Switzerland was to enable the company to make a secondary offering to enlarge the circle of Guinness shareholders internationally. Bank Leu definitely did not engage in any insider transactions in the agreement with Guinness. Prior to publication of reports on this subject in the UK press late last year our bank had no cause to doubt that the Guinness board of directors had been duly informed of the respective transactions.'

At the same time as this statement was released, Artur Furer, chairman of the bank's supervisory board and a director of Guinness, resigned his Guinness directorship. He said that the new chairman, Sir Norman Macfarlane, had assured him he was not suspected of any impropriety. Sir Norman made no comment.

## 'Wool of bat and tongue of dog'

The Companies Act 1985 prohibits a company from buying back its own shares or from giving any form of financial assistance for the purchase of its own shares, except in limited circumstances. Any company director 'in default' of that prohibition may, on conviction, be fined or jailed. Ward and Roux had now been named by Guinness themselves in a letter to shareholders, 'signed on its behalf by Mr Ward or Mr Roux'. Not surprisingly, Roux's solicitors issued a statement 'to protect his legal position' claiming that he did not enter into the buy-back arrangements with Bank Leu until June, two months after the end of the takeover battle.

No one could find Ward but everyone assumed he had retreated rapidly to the United States. Faced with all of this the Guinness share price fell to 271p, 59p lower than on 1st December, and the shareholders were warned that the interim dividend was likely to be postponed. Shareholders, if their memories could stretch back across the ocean of revelation, accusation and counter-accusation, must by now have been wondering why on earth they had not listened to the voices of reason the previous summer (even if some of them did come from Scotland) instead of the voices of hysteria and hype (most of which, regrettably, came from England).

The losses involved were now beginning to look alarming even for a company with a £2.5 billion capitalisation. To begin with the full amount of the Boesky US $100 million was now looking in jeopardy.

32. Michael Howard, Minister, Consumer Affairs. Because of Paul Channon's family connection he masterminded the investigation.

33. David Wynne Morgan, managing director, PR consultants, Hill and Knowlton. He took on an impossible task.

34.  David Donaldson QC, the legal side of the Department of Trade investigation.

35.  Sir David Napley, well-known lawyer. Many were surprised that Saunders appointed him. Sir Norman Macfarlane soon terminated the relationship with Guinness.

36. Dr Artur Furer, a director of Guinness and chairman of the Bank Leu in Switzerland. He protested his ignorance and innocence.

37. Gerald Ronson, chairman of Heron International. 'Mr Ronson's revelations must rank among the most amazing confessions ever to appear over a ticker tape machine.'

38.   Christopher Reeves, chief executive, Morgan Grenfell. 'Merchant banking is all about innovation . . . we must not believe that rules are written in tablets of stone'.

39. Graham Walsh, head of
corporate finance, Morgan
Grenfell. Damned if he knew
what was going on and damned
if he didn't.

40. Sir Peter Carey,
chairman, Morgan
Grenfell, former civil
servant. His task was to
clean out the stables.

41. and 42.   Shaun Dowling (above)
and Brian Baldcock (right) executive
directors of Guinness. The Roux
revelations about Saunders were
finally too much for them.

43.   Victor Steel,
executive director of
Guinness. The Roux
revelations about
Saunders were finally
too much for him too.

44.   Sir Jack Lyons,
Bain's man in London.
A recipient of fees from
Guinness.

45. Roger Seelig, director of corporate finance at Morgan Grenfell. A brilliant innovator in bid situations. Should he take all the blame? The Bank of England thought not.

On the Bank Leu indemnity the company faced a loss of £32 million given the fall in the Guinness share price. Furthermore, if the deal with Bank Leu was unlawful, as it appeared to be, then the £50 million deposit could be at risk as well. And constantly in the background there lurked the threat of a suit for damages from Argyll.

Where was it all going to end? What other indemnities and pay-outs were there? We did not have to wait long to find out. The auditors, Price Waterhouse, were already making threatening noises about invoices totalling £25 million that did not appear to be for pen nibs or carbon paper.

### 'Adder's fork and blind-worm's sting'

On Tuesday 20th January 1987 Clive Wolman in the *Financial Times* under the headline, 'Guinness share buyer won car fleet contract', revealed that Gerald Ronson's Heron Corporation had been awarded the contract for the management and maintenance of the 300 Guinness and Distillers' car fleets. Wolman also revealed that Ronson had been a heavy buyer of Guinness shares in the final stages of the takeover. Wolman continued in the article to discuss the figure of £25 million paid in fees which were a mystery to the new management and also the Schenley deal, 'The company is also investigating the transfer in November of the Dewar's whisky trademark in the US to Schenley Industries, the company owned by Meshulam Riklis which was a heavy purchaser of Guinness shares during the takeover bid. Guinness has not yet determined whether the trademark, which can be recalled in limited circumstances, would have commanded a significant price had it been sold on an arm's length basis.'

Having been caught with the sweets in his hand, as it were, Ronson decided that he better give them back. Lex, as usual, put it nicely, 'Mr Ronson's revelations—£5 million received from Guinness for services rendered, £0.8 million for losses sustained—must rank among the most amazing confessions ever to appear over a ticker tape machine. Merely sending the money back, the most complete act of contrition yet attempted by anyone involved in the entire scandal, seems unlikely to deflect questions about what Heron, and Guinness, thought they were doing in the first place.'

As one merchant banker put it, succinctly, 'As a straightforward banking proposition he would be entitled to a fee of, say £50,000. What did he consider he was doing to get a fee of £5 million?'

Ronson had sent a long letter to Sir Norman Macfarlane following Wolman's revelations. He implicated others in what was clearly a potentially illegal deal. ' It was also agreed that in the event of the Guinness bid being successful we would receive a success fee of £5 million. These arrangements were expressly confirmed to me by Mr Saunders. A representative of eminent brokers called on me to seek Heron's support.' Everyone of course immediately speculated on who the 'eminent brokers' might be. At the time of the bid Guinness' brokers had been Wood Mackenzie and Cazenove. You will remember that Wood Mackenzie had been one of the very few institutions to show that principle mattered as well as profit and had resigned the previous July. They were quick to show it was not them. Cazenove also denied the connection. Who then?

## 'Lizard's leg and howlet's wing'

The representative of eminent brokers was none other than Tony Parnes, known to his friends as 'the animal' and the 'eminent brokers' were therefore Alexanders, Laing and Cruickshank. (Oh my god! groaned the shareholders. There's no chance we could have that extraordinary general meeting again, is there?)

Alexanders, Laing and Cruickshank, who had been happy to take their half share of Parnes' very considerable dealings over the years— he was what is called a 'half-commission' man which means he uses their name and their facilities and splits his commission with them— immediately dropped him as though he were a scalding hot plate. 'At no time was A, L and C involved in any of these discussions with Mr Ronson and A, L and C did not then or at any other time advise Guinness.' Strange, Argyll had identified Alexander, Laing and Cruickshank and Cazenove as the two big buyers of Guinness shares in the crucial period at the end of the bid. And who, someone might have asked, made out the contract notes for Parnes' purchases on belalf of Ronson?

Parnes was a shadowy figure. None of the newspapers could even produce a photograph of him. They had to be content with photographs of his house, sorry mansion, in Hampstead. His nickname the 'animal' conjured up visions of King Kong but in fact referred to his habit of pacing up and down with a telephone to each ear and to each end of his mouth.

The imagination can run riot on the exchanges.

## 'Round about the cauldron go'

The names of all the recipients of the £25 million paid in fees were now revealed. As well as Heron and its £5.8 million, there was Morgan Grenfell with £1.65 million, J. Lyons Chamberlayne with £300,000, Zentralsparkasse und Kommerzial Bank with £254,000, CIFCO with £1.94 million, Consultations et Investissements with £3.35 million, Erlanger with £1.5 million, Konsultat SA with £3 million, Marketing and Acquisitions Consultants with £5.2 million and Rudani Corporation with £1.953 million.

Next to come forward after Ronson with an offer to repay was Ephraim Margulies, the chairman of S and W Berisford, the owners of Erlanger. His American subsidiary, Berisford Capital, had bought 2.8 million shares during the takeover, but according to Margulies the £1.5 million had been paid for work they might do in connection with future barter deals though Guinness themselves had suggested the wording on the invoice, 'Work in connection with the acquisition of Distillers'. Margulies also told Sir Norman Macfarlane in his letter offering to return the money, that the barter deal had been set up in a meeting with Tom Ward in Washington in June.

More intriguing than Margulies' involvement was the relatively small £300,000 paid to J. Lyons Chamberlayne. This company had been set up by Sir Jack Lyons and Major Nigel Chamberlayne-Macdonald. Its directors also include none other than Tony Parnes. Chamberlayne-Macdonald was once chairman of the Grosvenor Group, recently taken over after a battle by Robert Maxwell's Hollis Group. He is also a gentleman usher to the Queen and former equerry to the late Duke of Gloucester.

Sir Jack Lyons, the former boss of United Drapery Stores, which he left, according to the *Sunday Times*, after a difference of opinion about insider trading, was also the English associate of Bain and Co. Certainly he no longer includes United Drapery Stores in his *Who's Who* entry. (They do keep cropping up—these less than full *Who's Who* entries.) What a tangled web! We can be sure that Margaret Thatcher read with horror of Jack Lyons' involvement. Only a few days previously she had been at a lunch organised by him at Bain's offices. This was an indication of his influence and why Bain and Co. used him. But not for long. In what was now becoming a well established tradition, they dropped him. Or at least, again in a well established tradition, the newspapers said they had dropped him. Sir

147

Jack said, 'I have been unable to obtain confirmation of Bain's intention to draw our relationship to an end. If they do not wish to avail themselves of my advice, why they communicate this to the press and not to me is a mystery.' But soon the £300,000 paid to J. Lyons Chamberlayne was to pale into insignificance as Sir Jack admitted he had been paid a large sum for, 'Valuable advisory services rendered to Guinness. As was to be expected the fees were substantial, in fact in excess of £2 million, and were set by Guinness.'

It now transpired that Sir Jack knew both Parnes and Ronson well—Parnes is a director of J. Lyons Chamberlayne and Gerald Ronson and Sir Jack Lyons were both directors of the loss-making First Computer, a high street chain of computer shops recently sold to new management by Ronson's Heron Corporation. So Jack Lyons received £2 million for 'valuable advisory services'. Bain and Co. did not like it. They fired him and not through the newspapers this time. Hot on the heels of this disclosure came further agonised grunts from the 'animal'. He had been paid £3 million through a Swiss company, Consultations et Investissements. We can imagine that Alexanders, Laing and Cruickshank did not like that, but they had already told him never to darken their doors again. Both Parnes and Sir Jack agreed that Sir Jack had carried out the negotiations with Saunders and Ward. According to *The Times* of 4th February, 'The amount of the fees was largely determined by an initial offer from Mr Saunders. Sir Jack's response was to ask for an additional 10 per cent—and Mr Saunders and Mr Ward agreed.'

### 'But I shall crave your pardon'

If Lex found Gerald Ronson's letter to Sir Norman Macfarlane difficult to stomach others were staggered, especially by the sentence, 'I did not focus on the legal implications of what had occurred, nor did it cross my mind that City advisers and business people of such eminence would be asking us to join in doing something improper'. One comment from the City was, 'He's been in so many takeover bids, he should know the rules backwards'.

And he certainly had been in plenty of takeovers—beaten in 1982 by Holmes à Court in the bid for Lord Grade's ACC, beaten in 1983 by Lord Hanson in the bid for UDS, beaten in 1985 in a joint attempt with Cannon to gain control of Thorn EMI Screen Entertainment, not beaten but heavily involved in Burton's bid for Debenhams where he supported Sir Ralph Halpern crucially at the last minute. Yes, Gerald Ronson had been involved in many takeovers. Paul Cheesewright in the *Financial Times* ended an article outlining Ronson's career with this rather unkind paragraph, 'For the future, if there is any difficulty at home, there is always the bolt hole of the Netherlands Antilles. The group's overseas assets have been transferred offshore, although Heron remains a UK tax resident.'

## 'Go, get some water, And wash this filthy witness from your hand'

In the meantime the once-proud Morgan Grenfell was seemingly tearing itself apart. If the senior management thought they had solved their problems by throwing Seelig to the wolves they were wrong. Seelig was certainly the most active of their deal-makers, but had not the chairman and chief executive, Christopher Reeves, boasted earlier in 1986, 'Merchant banking is all about innovation. . . . We must not believe that rules are written in tablets of stone.' The establishment now wanted not just the head of the smart deal-maker but also of the people who authorised his activities.

In December, Christopher Reeves had said that the DTI investigation, 'Is not an investigation into Morgan Grenfell; it's an investigation into Guinness'. Officially this was so, but as the ripples spread and the prattlers prattled it was rapidly becoming an investigation into a lot of Guinness' erstwhile friends. Seelig had been treated by his superiors as though his tactics were at best unacceptable.

By Sunday 4th January the *Sunday Times* ran a full page article on Morgan Grenfell and it too wondered how long it could be before more heads rolled. By 13th January the bank appointed a committee of its own directors to look into its organisation and management controls. It would 'not be a witch hunt and not a whitewash'. By 18th January Christopher Reeves and Graham Walsh, head of corporate finance, were denying they were going to resign. Lord Catto had written to shareholders telling them that Seelig, 'Had not complied with the group's established practices and procedures for the conduct of such proceedings.' By 20th January Reeves and Walsh had resigned 'damned if they knew what was going on and damned for looking pretty silly if they did not'.

In the end it had required intervention by Nigel Lawson the Chancellor of the Exchequer, and Robin Leigh Pemberton, the Governor of the Bank of England, to force the resignations. 1987 was almost certainly going to be an election year and the Tories could not afford to be seen condoning malpractices amongst their 'friends' in the City. In the House of Commons Lawson talked of a tough policy for regulating City markets and warned of prosecutions in the Guinness affair, if necessary before the completion of the DTI report. Lawson said it was the Government and the Bank of England who were controlling the inquiry at Morgan Grenfell. The Bank, 'was closely involved in setting up and determining the terms of reference of the high level internal inquiry. . . . Any information suggesting criminal activity will, of course, be passed promptly to the appropriate authorities. In particular, the Bank of England is keeping me and the Department of Trade and Industry fully informed.'

Morgan Grenfell had become a victim of its own success. It had grown phenomenally fast since its 'second division' days in the 1970s, but that very growth and the encouragement the bank gave to stars such as Seelig (dismissed for not complying with established practices) brought it into disrepute. In the spring of 1986, at the height of the Distillers bid battle, Morgan Grenfell bought £180 million of Distillers' shares for Guinness. The Bank of England ruled that banks could not expose more than 25 per cent of their capital in buying shares for a client during a takeover. Morgan Grenfell's response was an effective thumbing of the nose to the Bank. It organised a consortium and carried on buying. That may have won admiration even respect for its gall but it did not make friends at the Bank. In January 1987 Morgan Grenfell needed friends at the Bank and not surprisingly found that it no longer had them. Bill Mackworth-Young, the former chairman of Morgan Grenfell (who died at the age of 58 in 1984) was probably turning in his grave.

### 'He was a gentleman on whom I built an absolute trust'

As the list of casualties lengthened the inquiring glances turned towards Cazenove and Co. Their reputation in the City and among major industrial companies was awesome. As one fund manager put it in June 1986, 'They're pretty arrogant, but they've got a reasonable amount of basis for so being. They are very high powered, they know what they're doing. They know exactly what the politics of various takeover situations are. They're the sort of people to have on your side in a deal, or very difficult adversaries if they're on the other side.'

It was this view, widely held, that led many to wonder how Cazenove could not have known at least some of what was going on. The DTI inspectors were said to be particularly interested in that purchase of 10 million Distillers shares (you will remember the vital 10 million that came on the market from Warburg Investment Management on 16th April 1986, two days before the bids closed) at 700p, 20p above the value of Guinness' bid. Any purchase by an associate of Guinness above the value of the bid would have been a serious breach of the takeover code. (You will also remember that the Argyll camp complained to the Takeover Panel who investigated the purchase. Cazenove assured the Panel that the clients who purchased the shares had no connection with Guinness.) With all that had since been revealed was this credible?

David Mayhew, the Cazenove partner who had been tipped to succeed senior partners John Kemp-Welch and Anthony Forbes, had been part of the famous Guinness war cabinet. By the last week of January of that war cabinet only he and Anthony Salz of Freshfields were still in place. Saunders, Seelig, Roux and Ward had been asked to leave. Could Mayhew survive much longer, particularly in view of his close friendship with Seelig? The Takeover Panel were already furious, not only because they had failed to find any trace of the £200 million share manipulation at the time, not only because of their weak handling of Saunders at the time of the Risk-affair, but also because they felt that Cazenove, this time in conjunction with Hill Samuel, had in their view broken their rules in the AE/Turner and Newall bid in the autumn. (The Turner and Newall/AE row was ultimately all about Barclays and Midland buying AE shares in the market and being *indemnified against any loss*.) 'The Panel is at a loss to understand how it could have been concluded that there was not a requirement to disclose given the breadth of the definition of an "associate" in the Code.' The Panel felt it had no alternative but to 'deplore' the fact that neither Cazenove nor Hill Samuel had consulted them.

### 'A weak, poor, innocent, lamb to appease an angry god'

Cazenove had a reputation for great secrecy. Indeed the magazine *Business* had written a whole article in 1986 entitled, 'The Secret

World of Cazenove and Co.'. Lord Faringdon, when asked why Cazenove never talked to the press, replied, 'It's just that we aren't very good at it. We get in a sort of muddle.' Well, the world was now expecting Cazenove to talk to someone and the air was rife with speculation that David Mayhew would be the next to resign.

On Wednesday, 28th January, Robin Cook, the Labour MP for Livingston and Labour's trade spokesman, accused Cazenove of being involved in the arrangements to drive up the Guinness share price. He spoke, of course, under the protection of parliamentary privilege. Mr Cook showed that on 6th May 1986, settlement day after the Distillers bid closed, Cazenove bought 20 million Guinness shares for Cazenove nominees. This was the same day that Morgan Grenfell paid the famous £7.6 million to Ansbacher, 'It is irresistible to come to the conclusion that the payment by Cazenove on the same day was for the same purpose, to pay back some members of the concert party who had bought Guinness shares on a temporary basis during the bid of Distillers to drive up the price.' Mr Cook went on to criticise the Stock Exchange for failing to act with one of its members as had the Bank of England with Morgan Grenfell. Is Cazenove, he wondered, 'too big, too prestigious and too influential within the Stock Exchange for the Exchange to take effective action against them?'

Faced with these accusations in the House of Commons Cazenove were forced to make a statement, and they did so the next day. In effect it said they had commissioned the solicitors, Simmons and Simmons, to supplement their own internal investigation when the allegations of wrong-doing had come to light in December. Simmons and Simmons' main conclusions were:

(a)   Cazenove were not involved in, or aware of, any illegality;

(b)   Cazenove were naive not to realise the connection between Schenley and Guinness.

In their statement Cazenove also answered some questions that they knew, or assumed, people were asking:

(1)   Robin Cook's accusation—refuted it.

(2)   War cabinet involvement—nothing illegal while Mayhew there.

(3)   Firmness of Guinness share price—perceptive investors.

(4)   Cazenove involvement in share deals—'it is clear that a very

significant number of transactions took place without our involvement'.

(5)   The £25 million pay-off deals—we were not involved except possibly Erlanger.

(6)   Boesky—did not buy shares in Distillers or Guinness for him though did sell Guinness shares after the bid for his companies.

(7)   Ansbacher—did not deal for them.

(8)   Placing of shares after bid—yes, but did not know of any illegality.

(9)   David Mayhew's future in doubt—'no, nor has it ever been'.

The most difficult thing to accept is Cazenove's supposed lack of knowledge about Schenley. Cazenove said it believed that Schenley had no associate status. If Cazenove were as 'on the ball' as everyone said they were, how could they not have known about Schenleys trading relationship with Distillers. This had been widely publicised in January 1986. Many found Cazenove's statement disingenuous to say the least. Some, under the circumstances, found its final sentence arrogant, 'We do not propose to make any further comments at this stage.'

### 'Fillet of a Fenny Snake'

The cleaning of the stables continued even if Cazenove showed their stall to be already clean. Attention now switched to that shadowy figure from across the Atlantic, Tom Ward. Everyone had noticed that he seemed to be involved in every action now under scrutiny. Ward was a partner in the Washington law firm, Ward, Lazarus, Grow and Cihlar. A graduate of the University of Notre Dame in Indiana (better known for its 'fighting Irish' American football team), though it has a good and old law faculty, Ward worked for several Washington law firms in the 1970s before setting up his own practice.

He first met Saunders in the battle to discredit those criticising Nestlé's dried milk sales in the Third World. You will remember that neither he nor Saunders nor Nestlé for that matter emerged from that episode with any credit. But the controversy did not appear to harm Ward and he set up his current practice. His partners were Cihlar and Grow, two lawyers with strong academic qualifications, and Lazarus who had worked in the White House under Gerald Ford and who worked with Ronald Reagan in 1980 and 1981. This showed Ward's ability to recruit highly competent people to work for him even if he himself preferred wheeling and dealing in business.

Ward maintained his contact with Saunders and became a consultant to Guinness when Saunders became chief executive. In early 1985, just before the Bell's bid, Ward became a Guinness director. 'From that moment on, Tom Ward was *de facto* head of legal affairs' said a Guinness manager. It was certainly a high profile position for a Washington lawyer.

Certainly from mid-1985 onwards Ward seemed never more than two inches from Saunders' elbow and by mid-1986 Saunders seemed almost incapable of moving without him (some have likened it to the godfather and his *consilieri*). When Charles Fraser wanted to see Saunders in June 1986 to discuss with him the proposed dropping of Risk, Saunders would not see him until Ward had flown over from America. Several of the leading opponents of Guinness in their battle over not appointing Risk last year, found reason both to hate and to fear him. Apparently his favourite phrase in discussing points which were the subject of disagreement was, 'I hope you've got a good lawyer when you say that'. Threats of litigation were commonplace and because America is a very litigious nation, seemed only too credible and frightening. Look back through this book and see how many times Ward has been mentioned in activities which are now under intense scrutiny by the DTI. The deal which gave Meshulam Riklis the Dewars' trade-mark for example, was done in his office, and although the new Guinness board are trying to get hold of the relevant documents to see if the deal can be unwound they are being frustrated.

Although in mid-January 1987 Guinness defended the transfer of the Dewar's trade-mark on commercial grounds they did stress it had been done on the advice of Ward's law firm. Market estimates suggested that the Dewar's brand name should have cost £200 million. Riklis also acquired the valuable right to distribute Gordon's gin..

Mr Ward himself quickly left for Washington when 'the Guinness hit the fan' and although requested to do so has refused to resign from the board of Guinness. Angus Grossart said that when Ward was talking you were always 'listening for the echo'. The inspectors were still inspecting, the newspapers were speculating and the police thinking about policing; were those responsible for extradition thinking about extraditing?

Extradition or not, by early March 1987 the new Guinness board had fastened firmly on to the £5.2 million paid to Marketing and

Acquisition Consultants in Jersey. Earlier there had been suspicions that Ward was in some way connected with this company and by the time Guinness forced a court hearing at the Royal Court in Jersey there was no doubt about it. The action was brought by Guinness asserting that Saunders and Ward had breached their fiduciary duty to Guinness.

In its defence Marketing and Acquisition Consultants (MAC) said that the £5.2 million had been a payment to Ward for 'consulting services' provided during the Distillers bid. (Earlier there had been claims that Ward had told Roux he was being paid the money for services in connection with the distribution of Distillers brands in the US. This story had obviously been changed.) The Court was told that the £5.2 million had gone through three banks on the island—National Westminster, Midland and Charterhouse Bank (Jersey). From Charterhouse, £3 million had gone to Union Bank of Switzerland and on to another bank, Finterbank.

In its defence MAC said that the compensation was for Mr Ward personally as distinct from legal fees paid to his firm.

'The level of compensation was agreed at an amount equal to £5.2 million, which was one fifth of one per cent of the value of the ultimate bid. In comparison with sums paid in connection with that bid to Morgan Grenfell (£60 million), Kleinwort Benson (£5 million), A.W. Bain and Co. (£17.5 million) and Freshfields (£1.857 million) the figure was fair and appropriate, having regard to the services which Mr Ward rendered and the success he achieved.'

Mr Peter Mourant, the lawyer acting on behalf of Guinness, claimed that MAC had not fully complied with a court order to disclose all dealings with the money. He talked of the £5.2 million 'whizzing round the banks like traffic whizzing round Piccadilly Circus.' The court ordered Mr Michael Dee, the director of MAC representing them in court, to give further details within seven days.

Guinness claimed that Ward had not performed services worth £5.2 million and some might have noted that the payments to Morgan Grenfell, Kleinwort Benson, Freshfields and Bain and Co. were all to companies where many people were involved whereas the £5.2 million was to Ward personally as distinct from legal fees paid to his firm.

Furthermore those who had been close to the company during the bid wondered how valuable Ward had been in the takeover. He was claiming the credit for unblocking the reference to the Monopolies and Mergers Commission of the second bid by the selling off of some brands. As we have already seen, it was Jeremy Lever and John Swift who produced this solution and it was Charles Fraser of W. and J. Burness who put Saunders in touch with Lever and Swift.

Many would question how an American lawyer with virtually no experience of English law or British takeovers could provide services worth £5.2 million personally on top of fees paid to his law firm.

It was also pointed out, that as Ward discussed his remuneration with Saunders in the week beginning 20th February 1986, details should have appeared in the offer documents. (We seem to be getting to a stage where what was promised in the offer documents did not happen and what did not appear in the documents did happen.) Clearly, as a transaction in which a Guinness director was interested, it ought to have been formally disclosed to the Guinness board and minuted. All the offer document said in relation to Ward was, 'Mr Ward is a partner of Ward, Lazarus, Grow and Cihlar, which will receive a fee in respect of legal services in connection with this offer.' The document also said, 'No director of Guinness has, or has had, any interest in any transactions which are or were unusual in their nature.'

Perhaps the secret payment of £5.2 million to an account in Jersey and on through several banks was not considered 'unusual in nature' in the Guinness of early 1986.

By Thursday 19th March, the new Guinness board decided that legal action was the only way to recover the money and issued writs against both Saunders and Ward. This brought the first public pronouncement from Ward since December 1986. He stated that the £5.2 million was his earnings and that after deductions to pay US taxes and 'certain expenditures' the balance was in his possession on deposit. He had offered to put the money into an escrow account, subject to 'expeditious' arbitration. The Guinness board did not respond to this offer which prompted Ward to remark, 'In litigation in the Jersey Islands [sic] and in statements to the press the company has continued to publicly engage in an artifically mysterious, international hunt for the money'.

# EIGHT

## 'This avarice sticks deeper'

**Not Finished Yet**

The Guinness 'scandal' is far from finished and we can therefore draw few conclusions. Perhaps, enough has happened and enough is accepted fact, however, for us to ask a few questions and suggest a choice of answers.

**The Tip of an Iceberg**

Are the misdemeanours at Guinness the tip of an iceberg that permeates the City?

Kenneth Fleet, presumably in a last gesture of defiance over Saunders and rather than admit he had been wrong, certainly thought so on Christmas eve 1986. He wrote in *The Times*, 'Mr Howard, for his own political sake and the skins of others, had better be right. Even if he is proved to have had good grounds for sending his inspectors into

Guinness, this inquiry provided it goes deep enough, will surely find that the inspectors' work cannot, nor in the name of fairness, should it, be confined to the activities of Guinness during the Distillers war.'

Socialist politicians, for obvious reasons of supposed political advantage, attacked the City generally for the misdemeanours of a few. Still living in an age when their paymasters, the unions, commanded huge battalions in the 'honest' tasks of bashing metal, the Labour party threatened dire consequences for those engaged in the 'dishonest' task of managing financial assets. Hattersley branded all in the square mile with comments about sleazy undercurrents of greed and corruption.

Prolonged bull markets always produce excesses as more and more people become greedy. Many can still remember vividly the 'asset stripping' and secondary banking scandals of the early 1970s. There is no question that the rules in takeovers were being pushed to their limits in several of the takeovers in the last three years. Furthermore, the new megabids and the leveraged bids have provided new situations for which there were no rules.

It would, however, surely be wrong to condemn the whole of the City for the avaricious and possibly illegal behaviour of a few. The City employs hundreds of thousands of hard-working and innovative people and has become one of the foremost earners of foreign currency in the country. It is one of the few economic areas in the country envied by others throughout the world. That is all the more reason why illegalities, if there have been any, should be brought to light and punished.

## Has the Law Been Broken?

Naked ambition and the cavalier treatment of associates and colleagues may be unwise long-term policies but they are not crimes in themselves. Clearly there was the strong suspicion that the law had been broken or the Department of Trade would not have sent in its inspectors. Enough has since been revealed either through investigation or genuine fear causing people to talk or return money to make it almost impossible to believe that some law has not been broken. How might the law have been broken?

Company law would have been broken if Guinness directly or indirectly bought its own shares without shareholder approval, even if this was only through an indemnity or an inducement to a third party to buy the share.

It would also have been broken if an arbitrageur had been given information about the imminence of a bid or a higher bid. This could have been done in return for support later in the battle. And the law would also have been broken if several parties had agreed to form a 'concert party' to purchase shares either in the bidding company or the target company without informing the takeover panel.

It is legal, for example, for a bank to buy a company's shares during a bid and indeed is now common, but if when the bid is over the merchant bank's fee appears excessive, should that be interpreted as a company giving financial help to buy its own shares?

Arbitrageurs are persistent and powerful people and certainly up until Boesky's arrest were considered, and indeed were, influential links in disputed takeovers. One banker put it succinctly, 'They ring you every day in bids and you certainly don't tell them to piss off because you need their support.'

There are many grey areas.

## Were the Authorities Weak?

One conclusion that could have been drawn in September 1986 after the Thomas Risk Affair was that either the rules for takeover commitments were wrong or that there was no one with the legal force or the strength of will to enforce them.

Until Saunders blatantly ignored a commitment made in a takeover most people thought such commitments were legally binding. Whatever advice they received from the lawyers the fact was no one seriously threatened to take Saunders or Guinness to court over the issue.

More lamentably perhaps, the guardians of fair play in the City, presumably the Bank of England, the Takeover Panel and the Stock Exchange did nothing of substance either. They passed the buck to the shareholders, effectively in this case made up mostly of either fund managers too young to remember the last bear market, or groups who were possibly part of an illegal concert party.

Thursday, 11th September 1986, the day of the Guinness EGM, was a day of shame for the City.

The Takeover Panel has been constantly criticised since its inception in 1968 especially at times of high-bid activity when new frontiers are being tested. As the world of business and finance changes so inevitably do the tactics and strategies used in takeovers.

The Panel is in the rather unfortunate position of having to react to each new situation without the benefit of precedent. Its rule book gets bigger and bigger. Indeed the Guinness affair has already caused it to grow again as the Panel has responded to criticism by tightening up the rules on disclosure, increasing its share transaction monitoring during bids and threatening to be more aggressive when it feels its rules have been broken.

The Panel is once again under heavy criticism and, depending on the Department of Trade and Industry report, could well be brought into some overall statutory control over takeovers and mergers.

The Bank of England has similarly responded to criticisms. The Governor, Sir Robin Leigh Pemberton appreciates that the alternative to a better ordered self-regulatory system will be a legalistic and therefore, by definition, less flexible system. As we have seen, pressure was applied to both Morgan Grenfell and Henry Ansbacher which brought resignations. The deputy governor, George Blunden said in early February 1987, 'Yes, we have been quite high-profile this last month, but we are happy to be seen as such in the cause of re-establishing the very high standards of the City of London.'

Was that perhaps a tacit admission that the Bank had been neglectful of its duties prior to this 'high-profile' month. Some might wonder whether more stringent controls were necessary.

## Will the New Securities and Investments Board be Effective?

Not even a statutory framework and body such as the American Securities and Exchange Commission will prevent more so-called City scandals in the future. The SEC, for example, did not prevent the Boesky insider dealing and other illegalities in the USA. Whether we have self-regulation or a strict legal framework in the City, people who want to break the rules or the law will do so. Because of the vast sums of money involved there will be the strong temptation to do so. Whether that temptation is resisted will depend on the perception of the chances of getting away with it.

One of the problems of the City of 1985 and 1986 was that the more aggressive and, therefore more rewarded operators appeared to be 'getting away' increasingly with practices which, if they did not break the rules, widened their interpretation with each successive bid.

The Securities and Investments Board, the new non-govermental watchdog of the City, have had due warning of the potential problems and will, we must presume, show its teeth at the first opportunity. If it continues to be zealous, and does not have the bad luck to uncover another major scandal, it will presumably be given the chance to operate without the full statutory backing demanded by those who want to see strict legal rules with swingeing penalties for those who transgress them.

The irony is that if a government, of whatever colour, brings in more stringent control, those aggressive takeover tacticians who craved the admiration of their fellows will merely have aroused their ire and indignation.

### 'To leave no rubs nor botches in the work'

Is someone going to gaol? Is someone even going to be arrested? It would appear incredible after all the revelation and drama if there were no arrests. The socialists would cry 'Whitewash!' Even the less doctrinaire would be tempted to tut-tut a little.

But company law and the breaking of it are complex matters and there would seem to be little point in arresting people unless there was a strong chance of conviction. Acquittal would bring even greater howls of anguish than no arrests at all. Some, though perhaps not many, would argue that many have already suffered enough through the disgrace. Others, as we have seen, want some very public executions.

We shall see.

# INDEX

# Index

# Index

# Index

Index

# Index

# Index

# Index

# Index

# Index

# Index